EXPAND
YOUR NET

BREAKING BARRIERS AND DISCOVERING YOUR
GOD-GIVEN POWER AND PURPOSE

PATRICE M. SCHAFFER

ISBN: 9798340256140
Independently Published by Theo & Patrice Schaffer Ministries

Scripture quotations are taken from [Bible Translation Used, e.g., New
International Version®, The Holy Bible, English Standard Version®], unless
otherwise noted.

Disclaimer: This book is a work of the author's personal beliefs and experiences.
It is intended for informational purposes only and is not a substitute for
professional advice.

For permissions, inquiries or booking, please contact:
info@patriceschaffer.com

FIRST EDITION: DECEMBER 2024

To my beloved Theopelis III,

This book is as much yours as it is mine. Every word is a testament to the love, patience, and unwavering faith you've poured into me through every step of this journey. When the nights grew long and doubts crept in, you were my steady hand, my quiet strength, my constant believer.

You've seen me at my highest and held me at my lowest, never once letting me forget my why. Your love has been my refuge, your laughter my joy, and your faith in me my light. I am forever grateful for the way you've held my dreams as tenderly as your own.

Thank you for standing beside me, for believing in me even when I couldn't believe in myself, and for making me feel like the most cherished person in the world. I couldn't have done this without you, and I wouldn't want to.

With all my heart and everything I am, I dedicate this to you, my love.

CONTENTS

INTRODUCTION

Casting Your Net on the Other Side

Have you ever stood on the edge of a precipice, looking out over a vast, uncharted horizon, feeling the weight of both excitement and fear? I vividly remember a moment in my own life that felt exactly like this. It was during a quiet evening, while reflecting on a recent workshop that had stirred something deep within me. The presenter spoke of a profound shift—between the familiar comfort of the past and the daunting promise of a new beginning. As I sat there, the realization hit me like a wave: I was standing on the shore of that very place. I could feel that I was on the brink of stepping into something far greater than I had ever imagined, but fear and uncertainty gripped me tightly.

This poignant experience led me to a question that I believe many of us grapple with: "What if the life I'm living is merely a prelude to something far more extraordinary?" This question is not just about seeking purpose but about understanding that the life we envision for ourselves often starts with a single, courageous step into the unknown.

This book is designed to address that very struggle. We live in a world where many of us are ensnared by limitations—whether self-imposed or induced by others. We are often held back by fear of failure, societal expectations, and our own doubts. The problem is that these constraints keep us from living fully and embracing our true potential. But there is a solution: embracing our divine calling and expanding our vision beyond the boundaries of our comfort zones.

The core message of this book revolves around the transformative journey of stepping out in faith. It's about responding to the call to "cast your net on the other side," as Jesus instructed His disciples in Luke 5:4. This call is more than a command; it is an invitation to challenge the status quo of our lives, to let go of what we know, and to trust in a greater plan that God has for us.

In the pages that follow, you will embark on a journey of profound self-discovery and metamorphosis. You will learn how to identify and overcome the barriers that have held you back, how to embrace the unique purpose that God has for your life, and how to navigate the path of faith with confidence and clarity. Each chapter is designed to build upon the last, leading you deeper into understanding and living out your God-given purpose.

How to Use This Book

Expand Your Net is more than just a book to read—it's a tool for change and growth. To help you get the most out of this journey, I've designed specific sections in each chapter to guide your personal reflection, spiritual insights, and practical application. Here's how you can fully engage with this resource:

1. Deep Water Moments

This section at the end of each chapter challenges you to dive deeper into the heart of the chapter's message. Through thought-provoking questions and insights, you'll have the chance to reflect on your own life, break down barriers, and apply God's truths in practical ways. These moments are designed to stir your spirit and bring clarity to areas where you can expand your faith.

2. Netting New Insights

In this section, you'll find key takeaways and fresh perspectives that are meant to "net" new revelations and practical application. These insights will reinforce the main themes of the chapter and help you intrinsically digest the lessons. Be open to what God is speaking to you through these insights, and let them stretch your understanding of His purpose for your life.

While there are no explicit journal prompts, every chapter allows you to personalize what you've learned between the deep water moments and the netting new insights section. I want to challenge you to journal during these times of awareness and revelation.

Writing down your thoughts, prayers, and reflections is a powerful way to process the transformative lessons and track your spiritual growth. Keep a journal close by as you read, and allow your reflections to lead you into honest conversations with yourself and God.

Truly Growing with This Resource

This book is meant to be a hands-on experience that guides you through practical Christian living and spiritual growth. Here are a few tips on how to maximize your journey with *Expand Your Net*:

Take Your Time: Don't rush through the chapters. Give yourself the space to reflect and candidly absorb the lessons before moving on.

Engage Fully: Dive into the Deep Water Moments honestly, write in your journal, commit to netting new insights applications and revisit the insights whenever you feel prompted.

Practice What You Learn: Apply the principles in your everyday life. Stepping out of your comfort zone and expanding your net will require faith, action and intentional practice, but the rewards will be worth it.

As you go through this book, remember it's about growth—spiritual, emotional, and practical. The road ahead will not always be smooth. You will face challenges, doubts, and moments of fear. But as you continue this journey, you will also experience breakthroughs, growth, and a renewed sense of purpose. You'll uncover the layers of your true identity and see the limitless possibilities that lie just beyond your current reality.

So, dear reader, as you turn these pages, prepare yourself for an adventure of faith and empowerment. The journey to expand your net and step into a life of purpose and power starts here. Are you ready to embrace the extraordinary and discover what lies beyond the horizon?

Let's set sail on this transformative voyage together, launching our nets into the deep and embracing the incredible potential that awaits us. The adventure begins now.

5 One day as Jesus was standing by the Lake of Gennesaret,[a] the people were crowding around him and listening to the word of God. 2 He saw at the water's edge two boats, left there by the fishermen, who were washing their nets. 3 He got into one of the boats, the one belonging to Simon, and asked him to put out a little from shore. Then he sat down and taught the people from the boat.

4 When he had finished speaking, he said to Simon, "Put out into deep water, and let down the nets for a catch."

5 Simon answered, "Master, we've worked hard all night and haven't caught anything. But because you say so, I will let down the nets."

6 When they had done so, they caught such a large number of fish that their nets began to break. 7 So they signaled their partners in the other boat to come and help them, and they came and filled both boats so full that they began to sink.

8 When Simon Peter saw this, he fell at Jesus' knees and said, "Go away from me, Lord; I am a sinful man!" 9 For he and all his companions were astonished at the catch of fish they had taken, 10 and so were James and John, the sons of Zebedee, Simon's partners.

Then Jesus said to Simon, "Don't be afraid; from now on you will fish for people." 11 So they pulled their boats up on shore, left everything and followed him.

Luke 5:1-11

CHAPTER 1

Recognizing the Voice

"Master, we've worked hard all night and haven't caught anything.
But because you say so, I will let down the nets."
Luke 5:5

Imagine the scene: the shore of the Sea of Galilee bathed in the soft, golden light of dawn, the first rays of the sun slowly rising over the horizon, casting a warm glow over the still waters. The disciples, having toiled through the night, were weary and frustrated. They had cast their nets time and time again, but the sea had yielded nothing. Their faces were etched with disappointment, their hands sore from the relentless effort, and their spirits weighed down by the crushing reality of an empty catch. Standing at the brink of exhaustion and disillusionment, they were not just empty-handed fishermen; they were men on the edge of an identity crisis.

As these men, caught in the tension between despair and duty, prepared to give up, Jesus appeared. Whew, that's enough to preach right there! Someone needs to be reminded that Jesus still shows up in the middle of the tension. In the middle of hopelessness and desperation.

His presence, though unassuming at first, carried an authority that cut through the early morning stillness. He spoke a simple yet profound command: "Launch out into deep water, and let down the nets for a catch" (Luke 5:4).

In that moment, the disciples faced a pivotal decision. Would they trust this Rabbi's words, even when it defied all their seasoned experience and logic? Or would they let their fears, doubts, and the comfort of their previous failures dictate their response? Their initial hesitation is something we can all relate to when faced with God's call in our lives. Like the disciples, we often cling to our own understanding, hesitant to step out of the familiar. Or many of us, prepare to step out, but only in the direction we've chosen. Recognizing God's call is often the first and most crucial step in our journey of faith. But how do we discern His voice amid the clamor of our daily lives? How do we distinguish His divine direction from our own desires and fears?

God's call is deeply personal, tailor-made for each of us. It is not always a loud, booming voice but often a gentle whisper, a nudge in the right direction, a persistent feeling that refuses to fade. Consider this: according to a Barna Group study, over 30% of practicing Christians reported that they felt God speaking to them through prayer, while others sensed His guidance through scripture or the wise counsel of trusted friends and mentors (*2021 State of the Church Report*, Barna Group, 2021). This underscores the varied ways in which God can communicate with us.

However, this study also reveals a sobering reality: nearly 70% of Christians do not experience God speaking to them regularly. This gap highlights a pressing need for deeper spiritual connection and clarity. For many, the struggle may lie in the subtlety of God's voice or in distractions that cloud discernment. Yet, God's voice comes in diverse ways—through prayer, scripture, or the wise words of others—each method unique and purposeful. Exploring these avenues can help us recognize and respond to His voice, regardless of the form it takes.

Let's look at the story of Moses in Exodus 3 as a powerful example. God called him from a burning bush—a miraculous event in the midst of an ordinary day. Moses, much like the disciples, initially responded with hesitation and doubt. He questioned his ability, his worthiness, and his capacity to fulfill God's call. "Who am I that I should go to Pharaoh and bring the Israelites out of Egypt?" Moses asked (Exodus 3:11). But God reassured him, not by erasing the challenges ahead but by promising His presence and power:

"I will be with you." Exodus 3:12

This divine assurance is echoed in Jeremiah 29:11, where God declares,

"For I know the plans I have for you... plans to prosper you and not to harm you, plans to give you hope and a future."

God's call is never void of purpose or promise. It is not dependent on our abilities but on His own faithfulness. It beckons us to trust, to move beyond the safe shores of our own understanding and venture into the deep waters where our faith can be stretched and strengthened.

But stepping into these deep waters requires more than just recognition of God's call; it demands action. James 1:22 reminds us,

"Do not merely listen to the word, and so deceive yourselves. Do what it says."

The disciples could have easily dismissed Jesus' command as impractical, just as Moses could have walked away from the burning bush. Yet, they chose to obey, despite their reservations. And in that obedience, they witnessed the miraculous—a catch so abundant that it nearly broke their nets (Luke 5:6).

This is the transforming power of responding to God's call: it takes us from the brink of ordinary and plunges us into the extraordinary. It's in the deep waters, beyond the safety of the shore, where God reveals His fullness in our lives. And it's in those moments of uncertainty and surrender that we discover who we truly are in Him.

So, what does this mean for you? It means that God is inviting you into a deeper, more expansive understanding of His plans for your life. It means trusting Him enough to let go of your own plans, your own logic, and your own fears. It means embracing the call to launch out into the deep, knowing that what awaits you on the other side is a life filled with purpose, abundance, and the fulfillment of God's promises.

The Disciples' Initial Hesitation and Our Own Doubts

This moment in the story of Jesus and His disciples holds profound meaning, especially for those of us who have faced situations where we've exhausted all of our own resources, wisdom, and strength, only to see no tangible results. When Peter speaks in Luke 5:5, his words are filled with the raw emotion of a person who has given their all and come up empty:

"Master, we've worked hard all night and haven't caught anything. But because you say so, I will let down the nets"

Peter and the other disciples weren't novices—they were seasoned fishermen, professionals who knew these waters intimately. They had spent years mastering the craft, understanding the rhythms of the sea, the best times to cast nets, and the most fruitful locations to fish. Yet on this particular day, their expertise failed them. Their knowledge failed them. No matter how hard they worked or how many times they cast their nets, the outcome was the same: emptiness.

Their fatigue wasn't just physical; it was emotional and psychological. The frustration of laboring through the night with nothing to show for it had likely drained them of hope. This feeling resonates with anyone who has poured time, energy, and passion into something—whether it's a career, a relationship, or even a ministry—only to see little or no return on that investment.

Failure, especially repeated failure, has a way of wearing down our confidence. Peter's response captures a universal truth: failure often plants seeds of doubt. When you've tried everything you know, when you've worked diligently and still come up short, it's easy to start doubting your abilities, your efforts, and even your future.

But notice what Peter says next: "But because you say so." Here, we see a pivotal moment. Peter's experience tells him that casting the nets again is pointless. His reasoning and expertise tell him that nothing will change. Yet, he chooses to obey—not because the circumstances have changed, but because of who is giving the instruction.

This is where faith steps in. Jesus was asking Peter to trust Him, even though every logical and natural reason pointed to failure. Faith often calls us to move beyond what we know, beyond what we've experienced, and beyond what seems reasonable. Jesus' instruction wasn't just about catching fish; it was about teaching the disciples—and us—something deeper about trust, obedience, and perseverance.

Peter's decision to obey wasn't driven by renewed optimism; it was an act of surrender. He essentially says, "Lord, I don't understand this. I don't believe this will work. But because You say so, I will." My friend, we are looking at the very essence of faith—acting not because circumstances have changed or because we feel more capable, but because we trust the One giving the instruction. This decision represents a willingness to trust in something greater than his own understanding, to move beyond his frustration and exhaustion, and to take a leap of faith even when it didn't make sense.

The empty nets that frustrated the disciples are symbolic of our own limitations. No matter how skilled or knowledgeable we are, there are times when our best efforts simply aren't enough. But in those moments of limitation, God's power is revealed. It is in our emptiness that God fills us, in our weakness that His strength is made perfect.

What makes Peter's response so powerful is that he obeyed despite his doubt. Obedience doesn't always require certainty. Obedience doesn't require understanding or even a changed mindset. In fact, the greatest acts of faith often happen in the midst of uncertainty, when our hearts and minds are wrestling with doubt and discouragement.

Peter's willingness to let down the nets again, despite his skepticism, teaches us a crucial lesson: faith isn't the absence of doubt; rather, it's choosing obedience and moving forward even when doubt lingers.This is where breakthroughs often occur—not when we have all the answers, but when we're willing to trust God in the face of our unanswered questions.

This moment of obedience led to an extraordinary outcome—a miraculous catch so abundant that their nets began to break. This wasn't just a catch of fish; it was a demonstration of what happens when we align our actions with God's word, even when it seems counterintuitive. The disciples' obedience unlocked a blessing that far exceeded their expectations.

Jesus' command to cast the nets again wasn't just a test of obedience; it was an invitation to experience God's abundance in the face of human insufficiency. The miraculous catch of fish that followed was not only a provision of physical resources, but a demonstration of God's ability to provide far beyond our human capabilities.

"Now to him who is able to do exceedingly abundantly above all that we ask or think, according to the power that works in us". Ephesians 3:20

How often do we find ourselves in situations where we've tried everything, yet our efforts seem fruitless? In those moments, it's easy to become disheartened and question whether we're on the right path. Doubts and fears whisper that we're not enough, that our efforts are in vain, and that perhaps we've misunderstood God's call. We begin to ponder if we heard God correctly, some even question, do I know the voice of God at all?

It is precisely in these moments of skepticism and reservation that our faith is put to the test. Like the disciples, we are invited to move beyond our fears and take that next step of obedience, trusting that God's wisdom far surpasses our own. When we do, we open the door to miracles—experiences that affirm God's presence and power in our lives, often in ways we could never have imagined.

In choosing to obey God's call, even when it challenges our logic and understanding, we position ourselves to witness His miraculous work. Our obedience, like the disciples', can lead to outcomes that not only bless us but also overflow to those around us. The story of the miraculous catch is a reminder that God's blessings are often on the other side of our doubts, and it is our trust and obedience that bridge the gap.

Deep Water Moment

Let us return to the shores of Galilee, where the disciples stood at the crossroads of doubt and faith. Picture yourself alongside them, holding your own net of dreams, fears, and uncertainties. Hear Jesus' call to you, inviting you to trust Him beyond your understanding. Your decision to read this book is a testament to the Father's gentle nudge—it is time to recognize His voice and follow. This is your moment. Recognize the call. Embrace the adventure. Cast your net on the other side and discover all that God has prepared for you.

Netting New Insights

Identifying and Acknowledging God's Voice and Purpose

To help you recognize and respond to God's call, consider the following exercises:

1. Prayerful Reflection

Spend time in quiet prayer, asking God to reveal His call for your life. Listen for His voice, and write down any thoughts, scriptures, or feelings that come to mind.

> *"For I know the plans I have for you," declares the Lord, "plans to prosper you and not to harm you, plans to give you hope and a future." Jeremiah 29:11*

2. Scripture Study

Jump into the Bible, particularly passages that speak to calling and purpose. Reflect on stories like those of Moses, Samuel, and Paul, and consider how God called them and used them for His purposes.

3. Seek Counsel

Talk to trusted Spirit-led mentors, pastors or friends who can provide Godly wisdom and insight. Sometimes, others can see God's hand in our lives more clearly than we can because "our greatness has become our normal," as Pastor Theo Schaffer would say..

4. Journaling

Keep a journal of your thoughts, prayers, and experiences as you seek to discern God's call. Writing can help clarify your thoughts and reveal patterns and themes in your life. This is also an easy way to see the growth within your spiritual journey.

5. Evaluate Your Passions and Gifts

Consider what you are passionate about and the gifts and talents God has given you. Often, our calling aligns with the unique way God has created us.

CHAPTER 2

The Language of God: Understanding His Voice

"God speaks in the silence of the heart. Listening is the beginning of prayer."
—Mother Teresa

As you begin this expedition of spiritual growth, one of the most powerful tools you'll develop is the ability to hear God's voice. Throughout Scripture, we see how crucial this connection is for believers. Whether you're making a big decision, seeking peace in hard times, or looking for direction in your life, God's voice provides wisdom and clarity every time.

In John 10:27, Jesus reminds us:

> *"My sheep hear my voice, and I know them, and they follow me."*

This speaks to the deep relationship between Jesus and His followers. If you're His, you can hear Him. But many people still wrestle with knowing how to hear God clearly. It can feel frustrating when life gets overwhelming, and it seems like His voice is distant or absent.

Dear Reader, if you don't remember anything from this chapter, please take this fact to heart, God is the master communicator. And here's the thing—God knows exactly how to communicate with you. As your Creator, He understands your unique personality, your struggles, and how you hear best. God's voice can show up in many ways as we discussed in Chapter 1, but let's focus on three primary ways He communicates: **hearing, knowing, and feeling.** Each one is different, but they all point to the intimate relationship He desires to have with you. Knowing these will give you the confidence to recognize His voice and start walking in the clarity He wants for your life.

Three Ways God Speaks

1. Hearing (Audible or Inner Voice)

God speaks directly to us, sometimes in an audible voice, though that may not be as common today as it was in biblical times. Even if you haven't experienced His audible voice, don't worry—He's still speaking. For many, God's voice can be heard in the thoughts that pop into our minds, similar to how we talk to ourselves. It's often hard to tell if it's God, but over time, we learn to recognize the difference.

Let's take a moment to remember Moses at the burning bush (Exodus 3:4), Samuel when he was a child (1 Samuel 3:10) or at the baptism of Jesus (Matthew 3:16, Mark 1:11, Luke 3:22). In all accounts, God spoke audibly; clearly and directly to people. The same God who spoke to them can speak to you too.

In my own spiritual journey, I've been blessed to hear God's voice audibly. It might sound peculiar, but this experience has etched itself into my heart, leaving no room for doubt. Picture this, when God desires to speak to me in a loud space: my ears warm, a hush settling over all the chaos like a stillness; as a call to attention to listen. It's not merely a physical sensation; it's an invitation to dive deeper into His presence.

I can still vividly recall those early moments in my life with God when I first realized that the voice I was hearing truly belonged to Him, rather than being just the murmurings of my own mind. In the quiet of prayer, it'd become easy to embrace the idea that God is guiding and present; however, in a bustling public setting, that certainty often felt elusive. After all, it's far simpler to brush off the supernatural as mere madness than to grapple with the awe-inspiring reality that the Creator of the universe is speaking directly to you, isn't it? It was during one of these crowded gatherings, surrounded by familiar faces, that I heard a voice whisper in my ear, "I'm going to use you in this space."

Turning to see who had spoken, I was met with silence—no one had uttered a word. I brushed it off, confused; feeling the warmth radiating from my right ear as I rubbed it for comfort. It felt strange, almost unsettling, yet the voice returned, repeating, "I'm going to use you in this space." Panic surged through me as I scanned the room, thinking, "Oh no, I'm hearing voices; I must be losing my mind." But then, the voice thundered, clear and authoritative: "Patrice, I'm going to use you in this space."

Before I could reconcile my thoughts with reality at that moment, a classmate crossed the room toward me forcefully, a look of urgency in her eyes. "I need you to pray for me," she said, catching me completely off guard. I mean, I'm wondering if I'm going crazy and how do I tell somebody I hear voices. Plus we had never spoken more than a few words to each other, and yet here she was, reaching out for help. I didn't have the luxury to ponder the significance of the voice—I had to trust that this must have been divine intervention.

I did the only thing I knew to do. I grabbed her hand in that classroom, the Holy Spirit surged within me immediately, and the atmosphere shifted quickly. As I moved according to the leading of the Holy Spirit; the glory of God swept through the room, and students began crying and repenting, enveloped in His presence. What started out as a simple gathering of the minds, concluded unexpectedly in praise and worship to the Father from students.

When we finished, she looked at me, her eyes welling with a mixture of relief and vulnerability. She explained how she'd been plagued by mysterious pains, the kind that had stolen her peace and left her family grasping for hope. They'd gone to the doctor, only to leave with more questions than answers. But before she walked out, a nurse—almost like a messenger—mentioned the power of prayer. In that very moment, she knew she had to find the girl that prays at school.

I stood there, frozen in awe, my mouth hanging open as I took in what she was saying. It hit me all at once—God had just worked a miracle right before my eyes, and He had let me hear Him in advance. The gravity of it overwhelmed me, like a surge of light breaking through fog. This moment changed me. It shattered any limits I'd unknowingly placed on God's voice, opening my heart to His willingness to work through me in ways I'd never dared imagine and surely not as young as I was.

You see, I had known Him in the stillness, in the gentle moments of prayer and intercession for others. But this was something else entirely. This time, He was guiding my every step, directing me amid the noise and rush of life. It was like standing in a whirlwind, yet hearing Him clear as day—an unmistakable turning point in my faith, revealing the God who doesn't just speak in the quiet but commands movements even in the chaos, shaping every moment for His glory.

Isaiah 30:21 tells us,

> *"Whether you turn to the right or to the left, your ears will hear a voice behind you, saying, 'This is the way; walk in it.'"*

God doesn't leave us to wander. He wants to guide us with clear direction.

2. Knowing (Inner Promptings)

Another powerful way God communicates with us is through a profound inner knowing—a sense that can feel as clear as words spoken aloud. Have you ever had a gut feeling about a decision, a gentle but firm sense that something was either perfectly right or completely off? We often say, "Something told me not to go that way" or "I just felt something wasn't right." Over the years, many Christians have settled for referring to this as intuition or just a gut feeling. For Spirit-filled believers, moments like these aren't just hunches; they are often whispers from God, guiding and protecting us in ways we may not immediately understand.

This inner prompting, that nudge in our hearts, is the Holy Spirit at work. In John 14:26, Jesus promises us the Holy Spirit as our Helper, teaching us and reminding us of His words. So when you feel an unshakable peace or clarity about a choice that defies logic, it's often the Holy Spirit guiding you. This divine knowing is a gift, a means for God to communicate directly with us in the midst of life's noise and confusion.

The Bible also speaks of spiritual gifts in 1 Corinthians 12—specifically the word of wisdom, the word of knowledge, and discerning of spirits—that enable us to understand life with supernatural insight. These gifts empower us to hear God's voice within and respond with faith and trust.

A compelling example of this is found in Acts 20:22, where the Apostle Paul describes being "compelled by the Spirit" to go to Jerusalem, despite knowing that hardship awaited him. This divine compulsion didn't come with a full explanation or guarantee of safety, yet it was so powerful that Paul followed without hesitation. Such moments of knowing transcend human logic, inviting us to walk in obedience, trusting God's purpose even when the path ahead is unclear.

As you open your heart to these nudges, remember that the Holy Spirit is ever-present, illuminating your way and drawing you closer to the heart of God. Recognizing and responding to His guidance will deepen your faith and lead to life-changing encounters, reminding you that God is indeed speaking—quietly, powerfully, and always with love.

3. Feeling (Emotional Responses)

Lastly, God communicates with us through our emotions, reaching the depths of our hearts in ways words cannot. This may be a deep, unshakable peace when we bring a matter to Him in prayer, or a stirring of joy, conviction, or awe when we worship. Scripture tells us of this profound emotional connection; in Philippians 4:7, Paul describes the peace of God as something that "surpasses all understanding," guarding our hearts and minds in Christ Jesus. When we experience this peace, it is often God's gentle way of affirming that He is with us and guiding us.

A beautiful example of God speaking through emotions can be found in the story of the disciples on the road to Emmaus. After Jesus revealed the scriptures to them, they said to one another,

> *"Were not our hearts burning within us while he talked with us on the road and opened the Scriptures to us?"*
> Luke 24:32

That burning wasn't just excitement or curiosity; it was a divine signal, a stirring deep within their spirits as Jesus spoke truth into their lives. It was as if the very truth itself was igniting their hearts, telling them they were in the presence of something holy and transformational—even if their minds couldn't fully grasp it. And here's the thing: we may forget someone's exact words, but we never forget how they made us feel.

This is especially true when it comes to how God communicates with us. He often speaks through our emotions, imprinting a reassurance that sticks with us even when our senses and circumstances tell us otherwise. When God stirs peace in your heart about a difficult decision or places a deep conviction in your spirit, it's His way of leaving a lasting mark, one that will stay with you even in the hardest moments. His language is often felt more than heard, inviting us to trust that He is present, guiding us, and holding us steady even when everything around us seems uncertain.

God uses our emotions not only to reveal what's happening within us but also to signal His presence and direction. Emotions can act as an invitation from God, calling us to pray, to draw near, or to respond in faith. For example, you may feel a sudden urge to pray for someone or a wave of joy that reassures you in the face of sorrow. These feelings, when aligned with God's Word, can be His voice moving within us.

God may also communicate through a conviction that settles deeply in our spirits—a call to action that simply won't fade. This might prompt us to pray for a friend, speak words of encouragement, or offer support to someone in need. As Romans 8:16 says,

> *"The Spirit himself testifies with our spirit that we are God's children,"*

affirming His presence and guidance in ways that resonate deeply within us.

Recognizing God's voice through emotions is a matter of sensitivity and surrender. When we invite the Holy Spirit to lead us, He speaks in the language of peace, love, and even discomfort—each emotion nudging us closer to God's heart and His purposes. Emotions, grounded in truth and aligned with scripture, can be powerful instruments for hearing and discerning God's voice in our lives.

Cultivating the Ability to Hear God

Hearing from God doesn't always happen overnight. It takes time and practice to learn to recognize His voice. But the more time you spend with Him—in prayer, in the Word, and in quiet moments—the clearer His voice will become.

As you go deeper, remember these three primary ways God speaks: hearing, knowing, and feeling. They're just the beginning. He also speaks through His Word, through other people, and even through circumstances. As you become more familiar with these different ways, you'll find yourself more confident in hearing and following His guidance.

One truth I've discovered about God is that the more you genuinely long to hear from Him, the more you will. It's like tuning into a frequency—you have to be willing to listen. A powerful reminder of God's desire to speak to His people is found in Jeremiah 33:3:

> "Call to me and I will answer you and tell you great and unsearchable things you do not know."

This verse powerfully illustrates how eager God is to communicate with you at every turn. So, open your heart and mind to the countless ways He speaks—through His Word, during quiet moments of reflection, and even amidst the chaos of daily life. His voice may come to you audibly, as an inner knowing, or through those gentle nudges that stir your emotions. Trust that He is guiding you to precisely where you need to be, filling you with insights and wisdom that will light your way. Remember, each time you reach out to Him, He promises to respond! Now, let's explore some of the other ways God may speak to you.

THE SCRIPTURES: HIS LIVING WORD

The first and most foundational way God speaks to us is through His Word. Hebrews 4:12 reminds us that,

> *"the Word of God is living and active, sharper than any two-edged sword."*

The Bible is not just a collection of stories from the past; it's alive and relevant, able to cut through confusion and guide us with clarity. When we engage with the Scriptures regularly, we grow in our understanding of God's character and His voice.

As 2 Timothy 3:16-17 teaches us,

> *"All Scripture is breathed out by God and profitable for teaching, reproof, correction, and training in righteousness."*

The more we know His Word, the more we recognize His heart for us and the easier it becomes to distinguish His voice and character from all the others.

THE HOLY SPIRIT: OUR COMFORTER AND GUIDE

God also speaks to us through the Holy Spirit, who dwells in us. John 14:26 promises that,

> *"the Holy Spirit will teach you all things and bring to your remembrance all that I have said to you."*

The Spirit nudges us, reminds us of God's promises, and gives us peace and direction in moments of uncertainty. Romans 8:14 says,

> *"For all who are led by the Spirit of God are sons of God."*

As we learn to be sensitive to the Spirit's leading, we become more in tune with God's voice, allowing Him to guide us in the everyday moments of life.

PRAYER: A TWO-WAY CONVERSATION

Prayer isn't just about bringing our requests and needs to God; it's also about listening. Think of Jeremiah 33:3 as a personal invitation from God to reach out and His promise that He will respond. When we take the time to quiet our hearts in prayer, we create space to hear from Him and invite His guidance into our lives.

Make listening a priority in your prayers—God often speaks to us in the stillness. When we allow Him the space to respond, we often receive direction in unexpected ways. One helpful model I use to balance prayer and listening is the P.R.A.Y. framework: Praise, Repent, Ask, and Yield (which means to listen).

When I first introduced this to my children, we would spend twice as long on the Yield part as we did on Praise, Repent, and Ask. So if we spent a minute on each of the first three, we would dedicate two minutes to listening. This approach not only helps you organize your prayers if you're unsure where to start but also creates intentional time to hear God's voice. Listening for Him is a skill that takes practice, but it's absolutely possible for everyone, and it can lead to a deeper connection with Him.

DREAMS, VISIONS, AND PROPHETIC WORDS

At times, God speaks through dreams, visions, and prophetic words. Joel 2:28 tells us,

> *"I will pour out my Spirit on all people; your sons and daughters will prophesy, your old men will dream dreams, your young men will see visions."*

These moments—whether through dreams, visions, or prophetic words—can provide profound assistance and confirmations as we seek to understand God's will for our lives. However, it's essential to recognize that not every dream, vision, or prophetic utterance originates from God. While these can be valuable channels through which He communicates, it is our responsibility to discern their source and ensure they align with Scripture.

To evaluate our experiences accurately, we need to ask ourselves if they draw us closer to the Father and glorify His name. If a dream or prophetic word doesn't lead us back to God or promote His glory, it's wise to question its authenticity. True messages from God bring clarity and encouragement, guiding us nearer to Him. In contrast, confusion and doubt may indicate that we are not hearing from Him but from another source. Remember, God doesn't want His communication to leave us feeling uncertain or confused.

In 1 Corinthians 14:3, Paul highlights the purpose of prophecy in the context of the new covenant—it's meant for edification, encouragement, and comfort. While prophetic words can indeed bring correction or reproof, they should always be rooted in these principles laid out in Scripture.

Lastly, it's essential to recognize the distinct difference between confusion and a lack of understanding. Confusion often breeds uncertainty and doubt, leaving us feeling lost and disoriented. It can create a sense of anxiety or fear, making it difficult to discern the truth. In contrast, a lack of understanding simply means we don't yet grasp a concept or situation fully. This recognition doesn't carry the same emotional weight; instead, it opens the door for questions, exploration, and growth.

Recently, I encountered what was declared to be a prophetic word that was not just overwhelming; it was exhausting. The entire experience left me grappling with confusion and emotional turmoil. What should have been a moment of revelation turned into over a week of wrestling to find spiritual alignment. Instead of clarity, I was met with more questions, doubt, and a sense of defeat.

When we find ourselves in a state of confusion, it can be paralyzing—leaving us unsure of how to move forward. But acknowledging a lack of understanding can be liberating; it encourages us to seek clarity and invites us to learn. This mindset prompts us to engage with others, ask questions, and deepen our knowledge. Rather than being stuck in confusion, we can embrace the journey of discovery, allowing ourselves to grow in our faith and understanding of God's will.

In spiritual contexts, confusion can hinder our relationship with God and prevent us from hearing His voice, while a lack of understanding can lead us to seek Him more fervently, opening our hearts and minds to His guidance. Therefore, distinguishing between the two is crucial. Embracing our lack of understanding can ultimately foster growth and lead us closer to the truth, whereas confusion can cause us to stray from it.

Proverbs 25:2 states,

> *"It is the glory of God to conceal a matter; to search out a matter is the glory of kings."*

This verse highlights that while God may conceal certain truths, He invites us to pursue understanding diligently. Our pursuit of His voice requires an active effort to search for clarity and wisdom, ultimately deepening our relationship with Him.

CIRCUMSTANCES: OPEN AND CLOSED DOORS

Sometimes, God communicates through our circumstances, using open and closed doors to guide us along the right path. This divine communication channel can manifest in the form of unexpected opportunities or the sudden removal of possibilities we once thought were certain. Revelation 3:7-8 beautifully illustrates this concept:

> *"The words of the Holy One, the true one, who has the key of David, who opens and no one will shut, who shuts and no one opens."*

This passage emphasizes God's sovereignty over our lives and the authority He possesses to guide our steps. When we encounter open doors, we are often presented with opportunities that align with God's purpose for us. These doors can signify His favor and affirmation, encouraging us to step forward in faith.

Conversely, closed doors may indicate that a certain path is not meant for us or a better one is on the horizon. Either way, this channel urges us to seek His direction further. By being attentive to our circumstances and recognizing the divine orchestration at play, we can discern the path God desires us to take. In addition to Revelation 3:7-8, we can look to Proverbs 16:9 for further insight:

> *"In their hearts, humans plan their course, but the Lord establishes their steps."*

This verse reinforces that while we may have our own plans and desires, it is ultimately God who directs our journey. Imagine the bumpers in a bowling alley: they guide the bowling ball toward the pins, preventing it from veering off course into the gutter. In the same way, God's guidance through our circumstances acts as divine bumpers, helping us navigate our paths and keep us aligned with His will.

Just as the bumpers redirect a wayward ball back toward the target, God allows events and situations in our lives to steer us in the right direction. When we remain sensitive to these nudges and adjustments—whether through open doors or closed ones—we can trust that He is helping us stay on course. By recognizing these divine interventions, we can move forward with confidence, knowing that God is actively guiding us toward His intended purpose for our lives.

GODLY COUNSEL: WISDOM IN FELLOWSHIP

In our quest of faith, it's essential to recognize that God often speaks to us through the wise counsel of others within our community of believers. This divine communication can come in the form of mentors, friends, pastors, or even fellow church members who offer insights and perspectives grounded in biblical truth.

"Where there is no guidance, a people falls, but in an abundance of counselors, there is safety." Proverbs 11:14

This verse serves as a reminder of the collective wisdom that exists within the body of Christ. Just as the disciples relied on one another for support and guidance, we, too, benefit from the wisdom of those who have walked the path of faith longer or who have experienced similar challenges. Godly counsel allows us to see situations from different angles.

When we share our concerns or decisions with trusted Spirit-led advisors, they can provide insights that we might overlook, helping us to discern God's voice amidst our own emotions or fears. Just as a ship needs multiple navigational tools to chart its course, our spiritual journey benefits from the diverse perspectives of our community.

Engaging with others also creates a framework for accountability. When we open our lives to trusted friends or mentors, they can encourage us to stay aligned with God's will and challenge us when we stray. The proper accountability fosters growth and strengthens our ability to hear God's voice clearly and consistently.

It is important that we lean on Spirit-led individuals to speak into our spiritual journey as others will not be able to give Godly counsel as Psalms 1:1 reminds us. There is safety in wise counsel. When we make decisions in isolation, we risk being led astray by our biases or emotions.

However, the collective wisdom of counselors serves as a protective barrier against misguided choices and adversarial attacks. Seeking advice from multiple sources helps us avoid pitfalls and navigate life's complexities with greater assurance.

Positioning Ourselves to Hear God Clearly

If you want to hear God more clearly, it starts with intentionally positioning yourself to listen. Here are some practical ways to cultivate that sensitivity:

1. Create Quiet Space

Set aside uninterrupted time with God. Psalm 46:10 encourages us to

> *"Be still and know that I am God."*

In moments of stillness, we quiet the distractions and better tune into His voice. Refer back to the P.R.A.Y. prayer model for how to structure this moment within your prayer time.

2. Engage with Scripture

Make time daily to read and meditate on the Bible. 2 Timothy 3:16-17 reminds us of the power of God's Word to shape our understanding and teach us. The more familiar we are with Scripture, the more clearly we will hear and identify His voice.

3. Practice Patience and Discernment

Hearing God takes time and discernment. Be patient—He will speak in His perfect timing.

Isaiah 30:21 tells us,

> *"Whether you turn to the right or the left, your ears will hear a voice behind you saying, 'This is the way; walk in it.'"*

4. Journal Your Journey

Writing down your prayers, thoughts, and impressions can help you recognize patterns in how God communicates. Habakkuk 2:2 encourages us to *"Write the vision; make it plain."* Over time, you'll see how He's been guiding you all along.

Hearing God's voice is a journey that requires practice, patience, and intentionality. The more we seek Him, the more we'll recognize His presence in our lives. Let's commit to positioning ourselves to hear Him more and trust that He's always speaking, guiding, and leading us forward in His love and purpose. God's voice brings peace, clarity, and direction—let's lean in and listen.

Common Misconceptions About Hearing God's Voice

It's completely natural to have doubts when it comes to hearing God speak. But let's clear up a few common misunderstandings:

"What if I don't hear anything?"

If you don't hear from God immediately, don't lose heart. Silence doesn't mean He's not there or that He's ignoring you. Often, silence is a powerful summoning to deepen your trust in Him, or He might be guiding you in ways you've not yet expected or experienced—through Scripture, your circumstances, or quiet nudges in your spirit. Trust that in His timing, He will make things clear.

"What if I can't tell if it's God's voice or just my own thoughts?"

Discerning God's voice is a skill you develop over time. The more you listen, the more familiar His voice will become—just like recognizing the voice of a close friend. God's voice will always reflect His Word and character. If you're unsure, test what you hear against Scripture, pray for clarity, and seek wisdom from trusted, Spirit-filled believers. It's also okay to ask for confirmation repeatedly. In the bible, Gideon asked God to do an impossible confirmation twice just to be sure. I would urge you to definitely get confirmation until you are sure it is God, especially when you want to quote God for the information.

"Does God only speak to certain people?"

Absolutely not! God does not reserve His voice for just a select few. In John 10:27, we are reminded that all of God's people—His sheep—have the incredible ability to hear His voice. This promise

48

is not limited to the spiritually elite or those with a specific title; it's available to everyone who follows Him and yearns for connection. God longs to speak to each and every one of us who seeks Him with an open heart.

Jeremiah 33:3 beautifully captures this assurance, echoing His promise that when we call on Him, He will answer us. Imagine that—God, the Creator of the universe, desires to have a deep, personal relationship with you! Part of this profound relationship includes the privilege of knowing and hearing His voice.

So, regardless of what you may have been taught, heard in the past or the lack thereof, take a bold step forward. Open yourself up to the possibility that hearing from God is not only attainable, but it's a vital aspect of your walk with Him. Embrace the truth that you are invited into this sacred communication, where His voice can guide, comfort, and inspire you in ways you never thought possible.

Growing in Confidence as You Listen for God's Voice

Hearing God's voice isn't about being perfect; it's about being available and willing. The more you intentionally listen, the more you'll recognize His voice—whether He speaks audibly, through Scripture, the gentle promptings of the Holy Spirit, or your Godly community. His voice is full of wisdom, truth, and love, guiding you toward His purpose for your life.

Don't be discouraged if it doesn't all come together at once. Like any relationship, learning to hear and trust God's voice is a journey. As you continue to seek Him, you'll not only hear Him more clearly but also find the confidence to follow His lead with boldness and faith.

Let this chapter be a stepping stone in your expedition to recognizing God's voice. He is speaking. Are you listening? It's time to lean in, trust His process, and walk forward in the confidence that you are guided by the One who knows you best. Keep expanding your net, casting it deep into the waters of His presence, and you'll find that His voice is never far from your reach. Don't let fear or doubt hold you back—God is waiting to speak to you!

Deep Water Moment

As we plunge into the deep waters of hearing God's voice, we uncover the boundless ways He communicates and the profound intimacy He longs for in our connection. Like the disciples, we find ourselves with our nets in hand, grappling with our own uncertainties, doubts and fears. In this sacred moment, we are called to embrace the depths of God's voice, surrendering to the stillness that invites us to listen. Here, we discover that in the act of truly hearing Him, we open ourselves to the fullness of our calling. Trust that His word is a firm foundation and He is truly eager to speak to you. God wants to illuminate the path ahead—if only you'd pause and truly listen. Let this be a time of reflection, where you invite transformation and insight into your life, fostering a deeper relationship with the One who speaks by simply saying, "Lord, I am here, listening."

Netting New Insights

1. Set Intentional Time

Schedule a daily quiet time with God, even if it's just 10-15 minutes. Choose a comfortable spot, perhaps with a cup of tea or coffee, where you can sit in silence, read Scripture, and pray.

2. Create a Visual Reminder

Write down key Scriptures that resonate with you about hearing God's voice. Create a visual reminder (like a wall hanging or a bookmark) that you can see daily, encouraging you to focus on God's promises.

3. Weekly Reflection

At the end of each week, take time to review your journal. Note any patterns, recurring themes, or instances where you felt God speaking. Reflect on how these insights can be applied in the coming week.

4. Engage in a Bible Study Group

Join or form a group focused on studying Scripture together. Share what you're learning about hearing God's voice and encourage one another to seek His guidance in your lives.

By venturing into these deep waters, we position ourselves to not only hear God's voice but to embrace the adventure of faith that He has laid out before us. As you expand your net, trust that God is actively communicating with you, guiding you into the fullness of His plans.

CHAPTER 3

Breaking Free from Limiting Beliefs

"Now faith is the substance of things hoped for, the evidence of things not seen."
Hebrews 11:1

The van jostled along the winding dirt road, each bump sending a vibration through its frame while clouds of dust erupted around us like a swirling fog. As we ascended higher into the Honduran hills, the landscape transformed into a tapestry of vibrant greens and earthy browns, each turn revealing a breathtaking vista that stretched out beneath the expansive blue sky. This is amazingly beautiful I thought as the enchanting terrain invited us deeper into the heart of the country.

Yet, I was crammed into the back seat of an old Toyota Sienna, surrounded by fellow believers; the air thick with anticipation. The landscape outside the window was breathtaking—lush greenery cascading down the mountainside, the sun casting a golden hue over everything. Yet, despite the beauty around me, I couldn't shake the tension tightening in my chest.

We were headed to a small village to deliver food to families in need. The plan was straightforward: introduce ourselves, hand out food packages, and offer a word of prayer. Easy, right? But deep down, I sensed that this trip was going to be much more than a simple mission of charity. I sensed the unmistakable tug of the Holy Spirit, a gentle yet powerful hint that something profound was on the verge of unfolding. While there were no audible signs just yet, the anticipation hung in the air like electricity, signaling that the Holy Spirit was poised for action, ready for whatever was coming next.

Long before this moment in the van on my first mission trip in Honduras, the Lord had been whispering to me during my prayer times, encouraging me to expand my net. Apparently, I desperately needed to change the perception of myself and the possibilities ahead if I planned to be a part of what God had already declared to be my future. He kept leading me to scriptures that challenged my limited perception, urging me to step into the identity He had designed for me. Time and time again, He brought me back to the same two stories, the disciples in Luke 5 and the story of Gideon, hiding in the winepress, yet still being called a mighty man of valor by the angel (Judges 6).

I was excited about this "new me" that God was calling forth, but no matter how hard I tried, I couldn't seem to shake off the old, familiar ways of thinking.

And here I was, in Honduras, on the brink of stepping into this new identity, but feeling the familiar nerves creeping up my spine. It was as if the dust swirling outside the van had settled into my thoughts, clouding my mind with doubts. Then, in the midst of my unease, I heard that still, small voice, whispering, "The only thing that's different is your location."

The words crashed over me like a tidal wave, leaving me breathless. My hands shook uncontrollably as my heart raced in my chest, pounding like a drum. How had I found myself at this moment? What had I been thinking? I felt as though I was sinking in deep water, far beyond my depth, and all the doubts I had worked so hard to keep at bay surged forth like a relentless tide. Each negative thought swirled around me, wrapping me in a cloak of uncertainty, whispering reasons why I wasn't capable of taking the next step that the Holy Spirit was urging me toward.

If we take a moment to reflect, we all know that inner voice all too well. It's not the voice of our adversary but rather our own thoughts—the ones that softly whisper doubts and fears into our minds. This voice tells us we aren't good enough, strong enough, or worthy of the dreams we cherish so deeply. While many of these lies are spoon-fed to us by the father of lies, plenty of them originate in our own minds. These self-limiting beliefs and negative self-talk become the chains that hold us back, keeping us from stepping into the fullness of our potential. But what if we could break free from these mental barriers and embrace a new narrative?

As the van jolted over a bump in the road, I felt the dust swirling through the open windows, stinging my eyes and filling my lungs. My fellow travelers were silent, each of us lost in our own thoughts, each of us hoping to see God move in ways that would shatter our expectations. And then, in the midst of the noise in my mind, a deep, unexplainable peace settled over me. It was as if God Himself had placed a hand on my heart, stilling the storm inside me.

In that moment, I was reminded of one of my favorite scriptures, Philippians 1:6,

> *"Being confident of this very thing, that he which hath begun a good work in you will perform it until the day of Jesus Christ."*

It was as if God was telling me, "You don't have to strive. You don't have to perform. I've already begun this work in you, and I will see it through." All the self-imposed pressure I felt to be "enough" melted away. The self-limiting beliefs that had plagued me—the fear that maybe God wouldn't use me in Honduras, or worse, that the things I thought God was saying were just my own imagination—started to lose their grip.

These weren't just attacks from the enemy; they were my own doubts, my own insecurities, whispering lies that I had rehearsed for far too long. Those subtle self-doubts had opened the floodgates, allowing the enemy to run rampant in my mind. Before I knew it, my whole body was sweating, and I was trembling with fear, doubt, and unbelief—not in God, but in myself.

But then it hit me: it wasn't about doing more or being more to become who God had made me. It was about believing that God was right, and that maybe, just maybe, I was wrong. Maybe the way I was use to God working in my life was too small, too limited. Maybe all the "great" things I thought I had experienced up until that point were just a glimpse of what He had actually planned for me. Maybe those experiences were actually stepping stones ushering me from faith to faith; glory to glory.

And as the Sienna pulled to a stop at the edge of the village, I realized something profound. The old me would have been paralyzed by the fear of failure, of not measuring up to the expectations I had placed on myself. But the new me—the one God was calling me to become—was ready to step into the unknown, to embrace the possibilities that lay ahead, knowing that I didn't have to be enough. Because God already was.

In Luke 5, the disciples faced their own set of limiting beliefs—not in a van in Honduras, but in a boat on the Sea of Galilee. After an exhausting night of fishing with nothing to show for it, they were ready to give up. In fact, they'd already made their way ashore to call it quits. These were skilled fishermen, yet in that moment, the very thing they were supposed to excel at, had left them empty-handed. Imagine the negative self-talk that must have swirled in their minds. The doubts, the fears—what if God doesn't show up? What if the gift they relied on fails?

But then Jesus showed up. Just as He met the disciples in their moment of doubt, I believe He met me in that van, on the brink of a downward spiral inside my own head, one that no one around me was even aware of. First came His peace, then His word, and finally, He reminded me of the vision He had given me when I was twelve years old:

> I saw myself standing on a stage, clearly an older version of me, and I felt an immediate connection. I thought, "Wow, she's amazing!" As I turned to take in the scene, I noticed thousands of people gathered around the stage, all trying to get closer, desperate to experience what God was doing. People were being healed—some by her touch, others simply by their faith. A man's limb grew back entirely, a woman's tumor fell out of her body, and a little boy was healed of cancer in an instant. I was speechless. It was an overwhelming sight, and as I tried to catch my breath, I heard God's voice, clear and with distinction: "Patrice, I've called you to nations." In that moment, I realized that every

person I saw represented not just individuals, but entire nations.

As I sat in that van, I couldn't help but wonder—could that vision still be true, even though this was my first foreign ministry adventure? I wrestled with the thought, trying to shake off the limitations in my mind. But all I could remember was that the vision had come over 20 years ago. Could it still be accurate, or had I somehow missed God?

When Jesus instructed the disciples to cast their nets on the other side, their initial response was one of skepticism and doubt as well. "Master, we've worked hard all night and haven't caught anything," Simon Peter replied. Yet, despite their reservations, they chose to trust Jesus' words and take action. In that moment, I realized I too had to choose to believe that God was right and that I was in fact, wrong about me.

Overcoming Skepticism and Doubts

The disciples' journey from doubt to faith offers us a powerful example of overcoming limiting beliefs. Like the disciples, my initial reaction was rooted in past experiences, or lack thereof and my own perceived limitations. Their unsuccessful experience led them to believe that their efforts were futile.

Even after holding onto a 20-year promise from the Lord, I had never ventured to another nation for ministry, and I still questioned whether that promise was truly meant for me. Our self-limiting beliefs often arise from past failures, fears, and insecurities. We convince ourselves that since we haven't succeeded in the past, we won't succeed now. Sometimes, we even project our perceived failures in one area onto our ability to succeed in another, creating a barrier to the possibilities ahead. But just as Jesus called the disciples to cast their nets again, He calls us to break free from the chains of doubt and embrace a new way of thinking.

Jesus' command challenges us all to shift our mindset and trust in something greater than our own understanding. If God has created me for this, and He has, then it's His task to make sure it comes to fruition, not mine. I must simply choose to partner with Him in it.

It wasn't until this realization landed on me like a ton of bricks that I understood: If this is my calling, then this is the very reason I breathe. This is the reason God continues to wake me up every day. This calling is more than just a task or a mission; it's the essence of who I am, woven into the very fabric of my being.

When I say it's why He wakes me up each day, I mean that each new dawn carries with it a divine invitation. It's as if God is saying, "Today is yours to embrace; go out and fulfill the purpose I've placed within you." The excitement of potential courses through my veins, and I realize that my existence is not random or without significance. Instead, I am part of a larger story—one that transcends my individual struggles and insecurities.

In essence, acknowledging that this calling is the reason I breathe reaffirms my purpose and motivates me to face each day with enthusiasm and determination. If I can't do anything else, regardless of where I am, I can definitely fulfill this call because it's what gives my life meaning.

Suddenly, my nervousness faded, and my confidence shifted from my own abilities to God's unwavering strength and consistency—the One who never fails. A new wave of boldness washed over me; I was ready to step into my purpose, intentionally and fearlessly, in a whole new country.

Deep Water Moment

Imagine the sun begins to rise, casting a golden glow on the waters, there with the disciples we stand but empty handed. In the distance, you've heard Jesus calling out to you. You're hesitant as memories of past failures flash before your eyes. But something within you stirs—a spark of faith, a glimmer of possibility is brewing.

What if this time really is different? What if, by trusting in His word and taking that step of faith, you could experience a breakthrough beyond your imagination? What if who I think He's called me to be is actually only a flash of the full picture of who He's made me to be?

Take a moment to reflect on the nets you've cast in your own life. Where have you experienced frustration and defeat? What limiting beliefs have held you back? Now, envision Jesus standing beside you, inviting you to expand your net—not in the same old way, but in a new, faith-filled direction following only His voice.

Are you ready to break free from the chains of doubt and step into what God has prepared for you? The journey begins with a single, courageous step: Cast your net on the other side and see what miracles await.

Netting New Insights

Breaking Free from Mental Barriers

1. Identify and Acknowledge Your Beliefs:

Begin by identifying the specific beliefs and thoughts that hold you back. Write them down and acknowledge their presence. Awareness is the first step toward change.

> *"For as he thinks in his heart, so is he." Proverbs 23:7*

2. Challenge and Reframe Your Thoughts:

Once you've identified your self-limiting beliefs, challenge their validity. Ask yourself, "Is this really true?" Reframe your thoughts with positive, empowering affirmations that align with God's truth about you.

> *"Do not conform to the pattern of this world, but be transformed by the renewing of your mind." Romans 12:2*

"Before I formed you in the womb I knew you, before you were born I set you apart; I appointed you as a prophet to the nations." Jeremiah 1:5

3. Embrace God's Perspective:

Replace your self-limiting beliefs with God's promises and perspective. Meditate on scriptures that affirm your worth, potential, and purpose in Him.

"I can do all things through Christ who strengthens me." Philippians 4:13

4. Take Faith-Filled Action:

Just as the disciples took action despite their doubts, step out in faith and take practical steps toward your goals. Trust that God will guide and empower you as you move forward.

"For we walk by faith, not by sight." 2 Corinthians 5:7

5. Surround Yourself with Support:

Seek out a community of like-minded individuals who will encourage and support you on your journey. Share your struggles and victories with others who can offer wisdom and accountability.

"Therefore encourage one another and build each other up, just as in fact you are doing." 1 Thessalonians 5:11

CHAPTER 4

Embracing Your Identity in Christ

"When you let go of who you think you should be, and embrace who God says you are, you begin to live a life of purpose that no one else can fulfill. Your identity isn't something to discover in the eyes of others, but to uncover in the heart of God."
—Patrice Schaffer

Discovering Who God Says You Are

In today's world, we are bombarded with messages that seek to define us based on external measures of success, appearance, and societal expectations. These labels often dictate inadvertently how we perceive ourselves, influencing our self-worth and shaping our identity. We may find ourselves striving to meet these standards, only to feel inadequate or incomplete when we fall short.

Yet, God offers a different perspective—a divine perspective that transcends worldly measures and societal norms. He sees beyond our external appearances, achievements, insecurities and flaws, looking directly into our hearts. In His eyes, we are not merely the sum of our accomplishments or failures, nor are we defined by fleeting social judgments and fads. Instead, God sees us as His masterpiece—His handcrafted creation, intricately designed and uniquely purposed.

Over the years, I've come to realize that showing up as your authentic self is invaluable—something truly priceless. I've become a fierce advocate for vulnerability and authenticity, but let me be honest, these strong convictions were born out of a time when I struggled to do just that. For a long time, I was so wrapped up in the roles others had assigned to me. They weren't necessarily bad roles; they just weren't "me". Sure, I was organized, but that didn't mean I wanted to be the secretary of every church ministry. And yes, I was passionate about the Word of God, but I couldn't settle for just being a vacation bible school teacher either. I was all of these things, yet I had no reference point for how to grow in them or where to begin.

So, I settled into what others wanted, defaulting to their expectations. It was easier, required less thought, and even less commitment. But here's the thing—it also kept me trapped in the very box I kept saying I wanted to escape. You see, my friend, you can't break out of a box without effort.

As I began to dig deeper into who God is, I started to discover who He actually called me to be. I'm someone who's good at a lot of things—not to boast, but that made it difficult to find my niche; identify my purpose. Have you ever bought a product for one specific function only to discover it has multiple uses? You end up feeling overwhelmed and unsure where to start, so you reluctantly consult the manual. That was me—too many functions, too many passions—and I needed the Manufacturer to guide me through it all. I knew in God's plan, He somehow planned to use it all, I just didn't know how.

I want to speak directly to anyone who feels like they haven't seen what God is calling them to do. This journey requires a close relationship with the Lord and careful instruction from Him. Without that, you might find yourself inspired by something similar and end up copying someone else, rather than authentically walking in who God has called you to be. It takes time, but trust me, it's worth the journey.

You also need a community that isn't preoccupied with finding a copycat of what you look like or something similar to what you do, but instead prayerfully encourages you to stay true to the original version God created.

As God began to reveal the reason for all the gifts, passions, and talents He placed within me, things started to make sense. At the time, I had never heard of the term "Revivalist" in the way God described it to me. He broke down every aspect of my character, failures, passions, gifts and explained why He created me for this role. Suddenly, it all began to click, and my calling became something I could embrace because for the first time ever, I actually understood it. I finally begin to grasp the profound truth of Ephesians 2:10—

> *"that we are God's masterpiece, created in Christ Jesus to do good works, which He prepared in advance for us to do."*

So, if you're struggling to understand or accept your calling, know this: God has already written your story. He's just waiting for you to consult the manual, so you can fully step into the role He's designed for you. It's not always easy, and it might take some time, but the process of discovering your true identity is one of the most fulfilling adventures you'll ever undertake.

Look again at Ephesians 2:10. This scripture unveils the depth of God's love and intentionality towards each of us. It tells us that we are not accidents or afterthoughts but deliberate creations with a divine purpose. In fact, God designed you as a solution to a problem. You are literally the answer to a prayer that exists in this realm. Oftentimes, we don't feel that or in some cases, even know it.

Understanding and embracing this truth is pivotal and life-changing. It shifts our focus from external validation to internal affirmation rooted in God's Word. It challenges us to reevaluate how we define ourselves and our worth. It commands us to confront every lie that seeks to overthrow God's definition of us. As we internalize the reality of being God's masterpiece, we begin to see ourselves through His eyes—valued, cherished, and empowered to fulfill the unique purpose He has prepared for you.

This embarkment of discovering who God says you are, requires intentional reflection, prayer, and study of scripture. It solicits us to let go of limiting beliefs and embrace the truth of our identity in Christ. As we align our self-perception with God's truth, we experience a profound sense of freedom and purpose. We are no longer defined by societal standards or limited by norms, but by our position as beloved children of God, empowered to live out His plan for our lives.

Ultimately, embracing our identity in Christ is a journey of faith and discovery—a passage that leads to a deeper relationship with God and a life filled with purpose and fulfillment.

You will not know the full picture of what God desires to do in you. Believe me, I've often struggled with the glimpses. However, understanding that the portion He chooses to share is contingent upon my willingness to pursue and determination to align with His will. God reveals secrets to those who seek them out. My dearest reader, this is a journey that invites you to cast off the labels of the world and "churchianity"; embrace the truth of who God created you to be—His beloved masterpiece, uniquely fashioned to reflect His glory and grace in this present space.

The Transformation of the Disciples' Identity Through Their Obedience to Jesus

The disciples' time with Jesus was marked by a profound metamorphosis of their identity. Initially, they were ordinary individuals: fishermen, tax collectors, and zealots, defined by their professions and societal roles. But through their obedience to Jesus, they began to see themselves in a new light; something and someone more.

When Jesus called Peter to launch into the deep, it was more than a command to catch fish; it was an invitation to step into a new identity, a new reality. In Luke 5:10, after the miraculous catch of fish, Jesus tells Peter, *"Don't be afraid; from now on you will fish for people."*

By trusting and obeying Jesus, the disciples experienced a shift from being defined by their past to embracing their God-given purpose. They were no longer just fishermen; they became fishers of men, entrusted with a divine mission. This marked a pivotal moment where Peter's identity shifted, the only thing is, Peter didn't quite know what that looked like, just yet.

What's profound to me is that the invitation to participate did not include a crash course of what would happen next, it simply offered an invite into the next moment but obedience was the first requirement.

This theme of transformation through obedience and encounter with Jesus is echoed throughout the New Testament. Consider the story of Matthew, the tax collector, who upon hearing Jesus' call, left everything behind to follow Him (Luke 5:27-28).

The newest tv phenomenon, *The Chosen*, does an amazing job of depicting Matthew's present struggles amid choosing to follow Jesus, forsaking all. He went from a despised tax collector to one of the twelve apostles, ultimately contributing to the writing of the Gospel of Matthew.

Can you imagine, one minute of obedience transformed his world and catapulted him into history. It wasn't easy but it was well worth it. Where will your yes to God in this season take you?

Sometimes we are so distracted by trying to discover the entirety of God's plan that we miss the first opportunity for obedience, "Follow Me." For me personally, this phrase is not just about leaving everything behind; it speaks more to trust. It's difficult to obey someone that you do not trust. Thus following is not even an option. But could it be that your quest for the end has caused you to miss the starting signal?

Embracing God-Given Purpose

Throughout the scriptures, we see that stepping into our God-given purpose often requires us to take bold leaps of faith, leaving behind the identities we've clung to, and trusting in the vision Jesus has for our lives. At the heart of the gospel is this very call—Jesus nudging us to forsake what we once considered normal and embrace a new identity that brings us into unity with the Father.

The disciples exemplified this truth. Despite their disbeliefs and skepticism, their willingness to follow Jesus changed them from ordinary individuals into pillars of the early Church, carrying the message of Christ to the ends of the earth. Paul captures this concept of embracing God's purpose with striking clarity in Philippians 3:13-14:

> *"Brothers and sisters, I do not consider myself yet to have taken hold of it. But one thing I do: Forgetting what is behind and straining toward what is ahead, I press on toward the goal to win the prize for which God has called me heavenward in Christ Jesus."*

This passage encapsulates the nature of what it means to embrace God-given purpose. Even Paul, with all his accomplishments, humbly admits that he hasn't fully grasped the entirety of his existence or purpose. This acknowledgment is crucial for all of us, reminding us that our faith journey is ongoing, requiring persistent effort and unwavering focus.

Paul's call to "forget what is behind" is more than just advice—it's a powerful directive. It's about making a deliberate choice to release past failures, mistakes, and even successes that could hold us back. In our walk with Christ, clinging to past identities—whether they bring us pride or regret—can prevent us from fully stepping into the purpose God has for us. For some, this sense of letting go is liberating, a breath of fresh air. For others, it's a daunting challenge, as it may mean walking away from things that once brought us fame, popularity, or recognition.

But Paul doesn't stop at forgetting. He emphasizes why this is so important: there's a prize we're pressing toward. Friend, pressing on toward the goal requires perseverance, resilience, and a focus on the prize of God's high calling in Christ Jesus. This heavenly calling isn't just about where we'll end up in eternity; it's about fulfilling the unique mission and purpose God has for you right here on earth. Pressing on means enduring trials, overcoming obstacles, and maintaining faith even when the journey is tough.

As believers, we must trust that God's plans for us are always in our best interest. Whatever He asks you to leave behind is necessary to make room for what lies ahead. To fully live out my God-given purpose, I must abandon all my fallback plans and wholly seek Him, following wherever He leads.

The disciples' lives are a powerful reminder that our identity in Christ is not fixed but constantly evolving. It's a process of continuous growth and renewal, where we are called to let go of our past and embrace the new life Jesus offers. As we follow Him, we too can experience the shift from being defined by our circumstances to living out our divine purpose, empowered by the Holy Spirit.

Deep Water Moment

Picture the moment when Jesus calls out to the disciples. He calls to the men but looks directly at Peter. This was not just about the fish anymore; it was about Peter's identity. Jesus saw him as a pivotal figure in the Kingdom of God although Peter saw only a fisherman. And in this moment, a failed one at that.

Reflect on the labels and identities you have carried. The labels you've placed on yourself for various reasons. How have they shaped your self-perception? Now, imagine Jesus, calling you by your true identity. I know you're hiding like Gideon, or suffocating in the box created by others, but this is not who I see when I look at you. I know you're doubtful Thomas, but I'm calling you to touch me.

In your journal, write about who you believe God says you are. Use scriptures to guide you. What new identities do you need to embrace? What old labels do you need to discard? Pray for the courage to step into your God-given identity and to live each day in alignment with His truth.

Remember, embracing your identity in Christ is a journey. It requires daily commitment to see yourself through God's lens and to live out the purpose He has for you.

Netting New Insights

Align Your Self-Perception with God's Truth

1. Meditate on Scripture

Spend time each day meditating on scriptures that speak to your identity in Christ. Verses like 1 Peter 2:9, which declares you are a chosen people and a royal priesthood, can help reshape your self-perception.

2. Affirmations of Faith

Write down affirmations based on biblical truths. Recite these affirmations daily to reinforce your new identity. For example:

"I am fearfully and wonderfully made" Psalm 139:14

"I am more than a conqueror through Him who loves me" Romans 8:37

3. Prayer and Reflection

Engage in regular prayer and reflection, asking God to reveal any false beliefs you hold about yourself and to replace them with His truth. Journaling your prayers and reflections can provide clarity and insight.

4. Seek Community

Surround yourself with a supportive community of believers who can affirm your identity in Christ and encourage you on your journey. Share your struggles and victories with them, and lean on their support.

5. Act in Faith

Step out in faith and act according to your new identity. Whether it's pursuing a new opportunity, speaking up for yourself, or serving others, let your actions reflect your God-given identity.

CHAPTER 5

Stepping into Purpose

"For we are God's handiwork, created in Christ Jesus to do good works, which God prepared in advance for us to do.
Ephesians 2:10"

Understanding and Discovering Your God-Given Purpose

Every person on this earth has a unique purpose made by God. Jeremiah 1:5 reminds us,

> *"Before I formed thee in the belly I knew thee; "*

In creation, God designed you as the answer to a need in this earth and handcrafted your arrival, oversaw your life plan and every detail to get you to exactly where He has need of you. His purpose is intertwined into the essence of who we are—your gifts, your passions, your experiences. Understanding and discovering your purpose requires you to listen to God's voice and be willing to step beyond comfort into obedience.

God's plans for us are often revealed through prayer, scripture, and the guidance of the Holy Spirit. Jeremiah 29:11 assures us of this:

> *"For I know the plans I have for you," declares the Lord, "plans to prosper you and not to harm you, plans to give you hope and a future."*

This verse is a cornerstone of faith, reminding us that God has a blueprint for each of us that is good and full of hope. The metamorphosis of the disciples from ordinary fishermen to fishers of men is a powerful prototype of stepping into God-given purpose. These men were leading simple, unremarkable lives until Jesus called them to follow Him. Their obedience to His voice changed the course of their lives and ultimately the course of history.

When Jesus called Peter, Andrew, James, and John, He said,

> *"Come, follow me, and I will send you out to fish for people."* Matthew 4:19

This was more than a change of profession; it was a call to a divine alignment. Despite their initial doubts, fears, and inadequacies, the disciples chose to trust Jesus and step into the unknown. There was no indication that this would work or that Jesus was the Son of God at this point but they still chose to trust. Their stories illustrate that stepping into purpose almost always requires leaving behind the familiar to embrace God's greater plan.

I already told you about my encounter when I was twelve. I didn't see glimpses of that fulfillment for many years and I'm still looking for the totality of God's plan. Why? Because there are many things that need to be developed, learned, exposed, forgotten, etc. New concepts, new imaginations and dreams that I haven't even scratched the surface of. Many times, we want to jump from start to finish and this causes much frustration in the interim. But the fact is, even the revelation that God has given, is only in part. Our understanding, interpretation and even performance requires His leading 100% of the way.

> *"Many are the plans in a person's heart, but it is the Lord's purpose that prevails."* Proverbs 19:21

This verse highlights a profound truth about the relationship between human intentions and divine sovereignty. It acknowledges that while individuals may have numerous plans and aspirations, ultimately, it is God's purpose that will stand. This verse serves as a reminder of the limits of human control and the supremacy of God's will.

You see, our plans are shaped by our understanding, experiences, and desires. Thus we interpret and expect God to move within the finite framework of our cognitive thinking. Consider me at twelve, ultimately, what I knew and understood at that level. It would be irresponsible of God to divulge an entire life plan yet alone more details to a child. I'll be honest, I still question how I managed to grasp what I did at that age but even that speaks to the sovereignty of God in knowing what we can handle.

However, the fact still remains that our perspective is limited at all ages. We can't foresee the future or understand all the variables that might impact our plans. In contrast, God's objectives are overarching and sovereign and exist despite our limits. It encompasses a broader viewpoint that includes His eternal wisdom and understanding of all things.

I don't want to belabor this point but let's look at a biblical case study. Joseph's Story (Genesis 37-50): Joseph had dreams that his brothers would bow down to him, but his path took unexpected turns involving those closest to him. Our dear brother was sold into slavery and imprisoned yet, despite these detours, God's purpose for Joseph—to save many lives during a famine—prevailed. Joseph would have never imagined nor would he have been able to accurately mind-map the plan of God to bring about this purpose. However, everything that happened, as readers of the scripture, we are able to see that it truly all worked for his good, even the bad. But, Joseph would have probably emphatically disagreed during and because of the process.

However, the truth of these scriptures and case study, encourage us to seek alignment with God's will, trust in His sovereignty, and embrace the journey He has laid out for us. By doing so, we find peace in knowing that our lives are part of a greater, divine narrative orchestrated by God Himself.

Perhaps you're still in pursuit of understanding your exact purpose. Let me share another profound nugget of wisdom from Pastor Theo, who emphasizes, "Purpose has a pattern." This statement epitomizes a key principle about discovering your God-given purpose: it often reveals itself through the consistent patterns in your life, particularly through the things you are naturally drawn to without expecting any reward. Usually the things that we are drawn to without pay, are in line with the problem God created us to solve.

For example, someone who has a ministry of help, they might find themselves miserable in a job that limits them to a specific task; however, they will find purpose in assisting others around them. A person who has a prophetic gifting, may find themselves always advocating for justice on behalf of a victim. They can be found cheering for the underdog in movies and passionately disgusted by injustice in church, family and society. Look over your life, find your pattern. You're not as far off as you think.

Imagine me, as a young pre-teen, trying to find purpose in life but also feeling God pulling me into the depths of something beyond my understanding. As a gifted individual, I found myself good at a lot of things but not fulfilled by them. I know what it's like to be made the youth leader simply because you're young or to be relegated to the secretary because you're organized. I know what it's like for the call of God to be far beyond your grasp or to even articulate. I found myself hungry for the supernatural things of God beyond human explanations but because of my talents; my family, friends and church community continued to handcraft boxes that further suffocated me.

I remember when the Lord first began to use me prophetically, around 12 years old. For my readers who may not completely understand that terminology, "prophetically" refers to the act of speaking or conveying messages that are believed to come from God. It often involves sharing insights about the future, spiritual truths, or revelations that guide, encourage, or challenge individuals or communities.

I didn't know how to navigate or have a current reference point for the call of God. Looking back, the thing that has been evident is that I have always been drawn to the supernatural encounters of God more than the institution of church as we know it.

This beautifully reflects the purpose for which God created me—to inspire kingdom thinking. I remember sharing this with a group of my peers when asked about my purpose, and their laughter filled the room. A highly acclaimed evangelist, and also a friend at the time, looked at me and laughed in my face, in front of a room of over 75 people, as he responded with a smirk in the microphone for all to hear, "What is that supposed to mean?"

I too know what it feels like for God to call and you struggle to articulate what you feel. I've been underestimated, laughed at, disregarded, dismissed, overlooked and mocked. I've had leaders and mentors to abuse and take advantage of my gifts and talents for the sake of propping their own ministries. I've had spiritual mothers and fathers, belittle me to remind me that God can't use me. Youth leaders declare that a desire for fame, popularity and to be seen were my motivators. I've had my own family displaced for the sake of man's personal gains.

To be honest, at the time, I wasn't even sure of what it looked like either; all I had was a word from the Lord. As I live this out, I now know that there are a number of ways to accomplish this mission but God continues to build upon this simple truth. When I preach, teach, mentor and am used by God, He always settles my heart with one simple phrase, "This is why you breathe."

Dearest reader, why do you breathe? Why does God wake you up every day?

Are you a kingdom benefactor? Are you a pastor? Are you a Spirit-led marketplace leader for a generation that needs to be reminded of our God? Are you a mother raising up giant slayers for the Master's good pleasure?

Your passions and talents are not random; they are distinctively linked to the problem God created you to solve. The unique combination of your skills and interests are designed to fulfill a specific need in this world. Your purpose is not just about you; it's about the impact you have on others. The things that you are naturally drawn to often align with areas where you desire to make a significant difference.

Did you know that true fulfillment comes when you align your actions with God's purpose for you? I was at a Pastors' Respite and the speaker polled the pastors, "Who is in the flow of fulfillment?" Most looked around to see who would be the first to respond while others checked for confusion. "What did he say?" The facilitator continued, when you serve others and address the problems you were created to solve, you experience a deep sense of satisfaction and fulfillment, it's called the "flow state".

In psychology, flow is a state of mind where someone is so immersed in an activity that they lose awareness of time and self, and forget about the world around them. In many other conversations, this concept is also known as self-actualization or self-realization. I didn't know any of the psychological names for it or even the ideologies but I knew I'd reached a point where I was exactly where God wanted me. It was easy to breathe and full of freedom. Hear me clearly, life didn't change and no bill collectors cared that I was in the flow. Life is still lifin' but it is definitely much easier being tired from doing what you are created to do versus what you are forced to do.

Understanding your purpose is a journey, and recognizing the patterns in your life can provide valuable insights. Take time to reflect on your natural inclinations, passions, and recurring themes, and by seeking God's guidance and engaging in service, you can uncover the problem you were created to solve. Remember, your purpose is intricately woven into who you are. Embrace this journey with faith and confidence, knowing that God's plan for your life is both meaningful and impactful. Today, I still don't know what the finale of Patrice Schaffer looks like, however, I'm definitely in the flow and I love it here. This book is possible, because of that flow.

Let's pause for a moment and revisit Luke 5. The disciples, seasoned fishermen, were dedicated to their craft, yet they were casting their nets for the wrong catch. What they truly needed was a shift in focus—to recalibrate their fishing skills into a mission for souls, becoming fishers of men. Through their obedience, they stepped out of the shadows of their past and into a vibrant new identity and purpose in Christ. This invitation is one that resonates with each of us, calling us to step boldly into the fullness of who God has designed us to be.

As we dig deeper into our God-given identity, it becomes clear that our sense of self is complexly tied to the legacy we leave for future generations. Our identity in Christ isn't merely about achieving personal fulfillment; it's about making a profound impact that echoes through time. In the next chapter, we'll uncover how embracing your true identity not only aligns you with divine purpose but also lays the groundwork for a lasting legacy that honors God and transforms lives. This flow of self-actualization isn't just a personal journey; it's a powerful movement toward building a future that reflects His glory.

Deep Water Moment

As we reflect on the disciples' journey toward uncovering their purpose, envision yourself in their position, holding a net brimming with your own dreams, fears, and uncertainties. In this moment, hear Jesus' call inviting you to step into purpose. This is your opportunity to trust Him beyond what you know, what you've experienced, and how you perceive your circumstances.

Embrace the adventure ahead. Cast your net on the other side and delve into the depths of God's purpose designed specifically for you. Remember, His plan often exceeds our reasoning and understanding. Just as the disciples transitioned from ordinary lives to making an extraordinary impact, you too are called to step into the extraordinary. You have the potential to create meaningful change in this world, and it all begins with the courage to take that step forward.

Netting New Insights

Practical Steps and Exercises to Help You Uncover and Pursue Your Purpose

1. Seek God Through Prayer and Scripture

Begin with a foundation of prayer. Ask God to reveal His purpose for your life and listen for His guidance. Spend time in scripture, allowing His word to illuminate your path. Dedicate a specific time each day for prayer and scripture reading. Keep a journal to record any insights or impressions you receive during this time. (Psalm 119:105).

2. Identify Your Gifts and Passions

Reflect on what you are naturally good at and what you love doing. These are often clues to your purpose. God has given each of us unique gifts to be used for His glory. List your talents, skills, and passions. Consider how these can be used to serve others and advance God's kingdom.

> *"Each of you should use whatever gift you have received to serve others, as faithful stewards of God's grace in its various forms."* 1 Peter 4:10

3. Examine Your Life Experiences

Your experiences, both positive and negative, can provide valuable insights into your purpose. God can use your past to prepare you for future ministry. Reflect on significant events in your life and how they have shaped you. Ask God to reveal how these experiences can be used for His purposes.

> *"And we know that in all things God works for the good of those who love him, who have been called according to his purpose."* Romans 8:28

4. Seek Counsel and Confirmation

Share your journey with trusted Spirit-filled friends, mentors, or pastors. They can offer valuable perspectives and confirmation of what God is revealing to you. Schedule regular conversations with a mentor or spiritual advisor. Discuss your thoughts and feelings about your purpose and seek their counsel.

> *"Plans fail for lack of counsel, but with many advisers they succeed"* Proverbs 15:22

5. Step Out in Faith

Sometimes discovering your purpose requires taking action. Begin serving in areas that align with your gifts and passions. As you step out in faith, God will guide and refine your path. Volunteer for a ministry or service opportunity that interests you. Be open to where God might lead you through this experience.

CHAPTER 6

Trusting in God's Plan

"Trust in the Lord with all your heart and lean not on your own understanding; in all your ways submit to him, and he will make your paths straight."
Proverbs 3:5-6

Trust is the cornerstone of our faith journey. It's the bridge between our limited understanding and God's infinite wisdom. At times, it also seems like the hardest piece of the process. Often inconsistent, seemingly impossible in moments. Hebrews 6 urges us that *"without faith it's impossible to please God."* (Verse 8) Whew, talk about demand.

I know I know, as we navigate the complexities of life, we often find ourselves clinging to our plans and timelines. The things that appear and feel more concrete and absolute. Yet, true faith and fulfillment come when we release our grip of control and simply trust in God's perfect timing and His plan.

In this chapter, we will explore the profound lessons of trust, still drawing inspiration from the disciples' journey with Jesus in Luke 5. They learned to trust Him deeply and in turn, witnessed miracles that transformed their lives and solidified their faith for years to come. Our voyage through the story of casting their nets is a powerful testament to the blessings that come from trusting God's plan even when we don't have all the information.

Trusting in God's Timing

My goal in this moment is to inspire you to embrace God's plan for your life while walking you through also embracing that His ways are truly higher and that His timing is in fact always perfect.

You see, trust requires surrendering our own expectations. Maybe you're a person who easily trusts God without warrant or maybe you're like me; at times trusting has felt like a force of hand while my back was against an immovable wall. I'm reminded of the first time I met Jesus as a provider for myself. Trust was the prerequisite and I wasn't completely willing to pay the cost of admissions.

You see, we sing the songs and read the scriptures, but His desire is for us to know His ways personally and not vicariously through others. In order to truly know Him as a healer, sickness has to rear its head up. I continued to recite the experiences of others, having no clue that God was about to give me my very own testimony of His providing power.

My freshman year in college at the University of Alabama (Roll Tide!) I was enjoying the "good" life. The access to Chick-Fil-A 24/7, on-campus and all the things I could get with my meal plan anywhere? Let me not forget my discovery of credit cards and T-shirts as a great exchange. Sure I'll apply for a credit card because that shirt is AWESOME and free! Yea, sounds ridiculous now but wasn't so obvious then.

I was living the life with what I thought was an endless supply of resources and freedom. No curfew, limited moral compass and plenty of opportunities to be free, whatever that meant. Whew, there are tons of stories in that year alone, including almost failing out of college altogether. Anyway, fast forward to my point.

You see, I'd recently had a come to Jesus experience, we'll talk about that later. I wanted to really grow in my commitment to God, but not just in words, as I'd seemingly become. I found myself in the middle of the unimaginable. My roommate turned bestie woke up on Tuesday and hated my guts out of nowhere. This was the same person that converted me to the doctrine of live your life and YOLO so I thought we'd die best friends. I mean after all, she was discipling me, right? To make matters worse, I realized that you actually have to pay the credit card bills, it wasn't free money. Who knew? Those T-shirts weren't that awesome after all.

My little campus job was trash and only bought gas to get back home to Birmingham to do laundry. I was broke-broke and all my funds were depleted. My parents after a turbulent few years were in the process of a costly divorce. I later realized that I was in escape mode, which led to some of my terrible decisions that year.

My older brothers were busy living their lives with one trying to repair the damage of his past while the other simply grasped for purpose. My youth group had disbursed and everyone was holding onto lifesavers in the middle of the treacherous sea of life. Not to mention a number of the trustworthy youth leaders had also recently created such a novel worthy narrative about my college experience from drugs to drinking, a true work of fiction that left me completely isolated and unknowingly broken. For the record, I wasn't being the best representative of Christ but I also wasn't doing any of what they said I was doing, yet. Anyway, stay focused.

I thought the guys chasing after me wanted more than a quick thrill—they seemed genuinely drawn to my personality, my time, maybe even my presence. I'd gained popularity fast, riding the wave of my connections with the high school basketball stars and as a UA football recruiter. It was thrilling, a rush that came without needing to compromise myself or give away anything more than a friendly smile and conversation. I was basking in the attention, caught up in the energy of it all. But even as I moved through the crowd, surrounded by voices and laughter, an emptiness lingered just beneath the surface.

In the noise and excitement, I was strangely alone—isolated in the very crowd that adored me. Beneath the surface of this popularity, I felt a quiet ache, a yearning for something deeper. I missed the Jesus I'd grown to know in my youth, not just in Bible stories, but as a real presence, a true confidant who could cut through the hollowness that lingered. Yet, my old friend seemed so distant, like a fading memory or a character from a storybook.

I found myself searching, sometimes in the stillness, sometimes in the chaos, grasping for a glimpse of the God who had once felt close. The God who was more than words on a page. I wanted to see His truth reflected in my life, in the here and now, amid the whirlwind of popularity and attention. I longed for His voice to quiet the noise and bring me home to something real—something that could fill the emptiness, not just mask it.

I remember this week so vividly. It truly changed my life. No money, no options, no resources, no people. I did the only thing I knew to do: I prayed and prayed. I mean ugly cried and everything but there was no response from God. I didn't have food to eat for a few days because I was a broke college student and had completely mismanaged everything I had access to. I remember rummaging through my purse, fingers crossing over loose change and receipts as I hunted for a forgotten piece of candy, anything to tide me over. I was determined to trust that God would provide, even though everything around me screamed uncertainty. In this strange mix of desperation and faith, I retreated to my car, my last refuge from a roommate who seemed bent on chaos and cruelty, as though she'd surrendered herself to something dark and destructive.

The sky was heavy, on the verge of a storm, and I could feel the weight of it pressing down. I imagined myself tearing through the glove compartment and under the seats, hoping for a stray cracker or a long-lost snack. At this point, I was scavenging, really, my pride unwilling to let me reach out for help, my fear convincing me that asking would only be a burden on others. I wanted to keep my struggle hidden, to bear it alone if I had to, all while silently praying for a breakthrough that only God could bring.

As I pulled myself to go outside, I ran from my dorm to parking spot 8. I found someone had attempted to steal my University of Alabama "F8thfl" car tag from my hunter green Honda Civic. My personalized tag was scratched, bent and hanging on by a screw, literally. Amazed and defeated at the same time, the rain began to pour and I fell to my knees in that parking lot and cried.

My tears and the rain mixed as I became drenched in search for solace from cares of life that I couldn't escape. I had reached the end of my rope and I was done. I didn't know where to go but I was done. I was over trying to pursue faithfulness and redemption in a God that only sought to make my life even worse than what it was. My eyes are watering as I write because I remember every emotion and thought that swarmed my mind as I found myself on the asphalt in that storm. I didn't even call out to God because He hadn't responded previously. As a person who has heard God audibly since I was 12, I'd never felt further from Him than I did in this moment. Even in sin, I could hear Him. Even when unfaithful, He always spoke. Even in the midst of chaos, I could hear Him. But here, I was listening and it was silent.

Then it happened, in the middle of the darkness storm, I heard God speak to me. Two words, "Trust Me!" I wanted to argue and buck back but I was exhausted. I hadn't eaten in days, had a list of reasons to give up but somehow felt a spark of hope in His message. I relate to the disciples in Luke 5 because although I wasn't in a literal boat, I know what it feels like to be exhausted and at the end of your rope. To want nothing more but to give up or go hide from the world because you feel like a failure. Have you ever just wanted to quit? I mean truly, maybe I'm not good at this. Maybe I'm not called or anointed for this. I keep failing, so maybe I heard God wrong.

In the middle of the endless noise swirling in your mind, each thought louder than the last, there's Jesus, trying to get through. He has to raise His voice above the clamor, calling your name with urgency, pulling you back from the overwhelming tide of worries, distractions, and doubts. It's as if He's reaching through the fog of your own thoughts, cutting through the noise just to bring you back to Him. And in that moment, His voice stands alone, clear and steady—a lifeline drawing you out of the chaos and back to His peace.

Before Jesus invites Peter to cast his net into the deep water, He calls his name. This personal address is more than a mere calling out; it is a moment of deep connection and recognition. Sometimes we're far too distracted and it's imperative that He calls your name to establish a foundation of trust and intimacy because what happens next, is going to change your life.

Despite their doubts and the futility of their own efforts, the disciples chose to obey Jesus, without knowing obedience would lead to the miraculous. This event not only transformed their profession but also deepened their trust in Him.

As I picked myself up from the asphalt, I returned to my dorm room drenched. I walked into our shared space and my roommate at that moment probably thought I was a lunatic for sure. At this point, I no longer cared what anyone thought. I went straight for my bed and just laid there.

I was completely drained, my eyes swollen and blurred from tears that refused to let me see clearly. Just as I drifted into an uneasy sleep, a sharp knock echoed through the room. For a moment, I sat there in a daze, unsure if I'd imagined it. But the knock came again, steady and insistent, pulling me from the fog of exhaustion and forcing me to sit up.

I glanced at the clock—two hours had passed. When I opened my dorm room door, a girl from upstairs stood there, slightly hurried but polite, holding an envelope. She explained it was mail for me, mistakenly delivered to her room. I thanked her, but I wasn't exactly eager to read another letter, possibly yet another credit card bill. As I set it aside, I felt a gentle nudge in my spirit: "You're going to want to see this."

With a sigh, but now a hint of curiosity, with the door wide open, I tore the envelope and unfolded the paper inside. My breath caught—it was a check for $2,000! But it wasn't just the money that stunned me. The letter came from a church I'd briefly helped out when I was 14 years old, doing administrative tasks as a favor to my pastor, the late Bishop Heron Johnson. In gratitude for my service, they'd awarded me a scholarship—something I'd long forgotten. And here it was, years later, delivered at exactly the moment I needed it most.

The postmark? Four days before, on the very day I'd made the decision to fully trust God with my needs.

Embracing Divine Timing & Relinquishing Control

Trusting God truly means canceling your evacuation plans. It requires abandoning the instinct to flee when things don't go as planned and instead, lean solely on Him. This kind of trust isn't always easy because it involves surrendering our sense of control and comfort. We often find ourselves ready for a breakthrough, eager for change, yet God, in His infinite wisdom, knows the perfect moment to reveal His plans. His timing may not align with ours, but it is never late. He shows up at the edge of the sea just in time to tell the disciples to go back out. For many of us, the ideal time would have been before they'd wasted an entire night catching nothing.

Ecclesiastes 3:11 reminds us, *"He has made everything beautiful in its time."* Trusting God means believing that He is orchestrating every detail, even when our impatience tempts us to take matters into our own hands because we think we have a better plan.

To rely on God is to let go of our need to understand every step and to rest in the assurance that His ways are higher than our own. We must release our grip of control, acknowledging that God's blueprints are ultimately for our good, even when we can't see the full picture. Isaiah 55:8-9 echoes this truth,

> *"For my thoughts are not your thoughts, neither are your ways my ways," declares the Lord. "As the heavens are higher than the earth, so are my ways higher than your ways and my thoughts than your thoughts."*

Trusting in God means choosing to stay the course He has set for us, even when uncertainty and doubt try to push us toward escape routes of our own making. It is in this place of surrender that we truly begin to experience the depth of His faithfulness and like the disciples, we get to see that God truly knows best.

Deep Water Moment

This chapter has highlighted the disciples' choice to trust Jesus and despite their doubts, timing and understanding. Picture yourself feeling depleted of resources and time, exhausted from the struggles of the night. Many of us don't have to picture this, we're standing right there in our reality. Yet Jesus allows us to come to this place only to hear His gentle call to trust Him.

But He's not a fisherman, they thought; but somehow, He seems to know what He's talking about. This is your deep water moment—a call to trust in God's plan and divine timing. Take a few minutes to reflect on areas in your life where you genuinely struggle to trust God's plan and specifically God's timing. Jot down your fears and surrender them in prayer. Ask God to help you release control and develop patience and trust as you wait for His perfect timing.

Netting New Insights

Practical Steps for Developing Faith and Patience

1. Prayer and Meditation

Engaging in regular prayer and meditation on scripture helps us to focus our minds on God's promises and develop patience. These practices allow us to find peace in the midst of uncertainty and wait with a hopeful heart. Set aside a dedicated time each day for prayer and meditation. Use this time to surrender your worries to God and ask for the strength to trust His timing.

2. Reflecting on Past Faithfulness

Reflect on instances in your life where God has proven His faithfulness. Remembering past victories helps to build trust for future uncertainties. It might be helpful to keep a journal of moments when God has come through for you. Revisit these entries during times of doubt to remind yourself of His unwavering faithfulness (Hebrews 13:8).

3. Community and Support

Surround yourself with a community of believers who can encourage and support you in your journey. Sharing your struggles and victories with others strengthens your faith and provides mutual encouragement. Join a small group or a prayer circle where you can share your experiences and receive support from others who are also trusting in God's plan.

CHAPTER 7

Overcoming Obstacles

"Hardships often prepare ordinary people for an extraordinary destiny."
C.S. Lewis

By now, we're familiar with the story in Luke 5. But let's shift our perspective and take another look. Let's observe Peter, standing at the edge of a significant obstacle—his own doubt. His story throughout the Gospels shows us a man who wrestles with doubt, insecurity, and impulsiveness often. Look at Him. He's a seasoned fisherman, fully aware of the waters and conditions, and every logical thought in him says the situation is futile.

His initial response is hesitation, a real reflection of what it feels like to face setbacks and challenges head-on. Yet, in that pivotal moment, Peter chooses to trust Jesus' command, despite his instincts and expertise telling him otherwise. His path demonstrates how God can work through our struggles and refine us through both our doubts and faith. It's a powerful reminder of the extraordinary things that unfold when we trust God beyond what we can see or understand.

Navigating Challenges and Setbacks

The life of a believer is not without its challenges. Obstacles are an inevitable part of human life, and the Bible is filled with stories of individuals who faced insurmountable odds yet overcame them by standing on God's promises. Remember our friend, Joseph, who was sold into slavery by his own brothers, falsely accused, and imprisoned. Despite these trials, Joseph remained faithful, and in time, God elevated him to a position of great power in Egypt, ultimately using him to save many lives during a famine (Genesis 37-50). His story is a powerful reminder that God can turn what was meant for evil into something good, even when the road seems impossibly difficult.

Similarly, the story of Ruth, a Moabite widow who chose to follow her mother-in-law Naomi back to Bethlehem, is another example of overcoming adversity. Ruth faced the challenges of being a foreigner in a strange land, a widow with no means of support, and yet she remained faithful to Naomi and to Naomi's God. Her resilience and loyalty eventually led to her becoming the great-grandmother of King David, and through her lineage, the Messiah would come (Ruth 1-4). Ruth's story teaches us that perseverance in the face of hardship and unwavering faith in God's provision can lead to extraordinary outcomes.

We all face setbacks, disappointments, and challenges. Many of us have a favorite song or routine that gets us pumped up, but while these can boost our motivation, true resilience requires more than a quick burst of inspiration. Overcoming obstacles means digging deep, building strength, and pushing forward with determination.

One of the most powerful ways to build this resilience is by staying grounded in prayer and immersing ourselves in God's Word. In Philippians 4:6-7, Paul advises us to

> *"not be anxious about anything, but in every situation, by prayer and petition, with thanksgiving, present your requests to God."*

In return, God promises His peace—one that surpasses all understanding—to guard our hearts and minds in Christ. A routined prayer schedule keeps us centered, infusing us with peace, clarity, and strength to face whatever lies ahead. It's a spiritual practice with real, lasting impact on our minds and souls.

When we pray, we enter into a sacred conversation with God, laying our burdens, fears, and anxieties at His feet. This act of surrender is not just a spiritual discipline but also a deeply healing process for our minds and hearts. Through prayer, we are invited to release our worries, trusting that God will replace them with His peace. This peace acts as a guard over our hearts and minds, protecting us from the overwhelming nature of our challenges.

Prayer doesn't just give us peace; it pulls our focus off the mountains or obstacles in front of us and fixes our gaze back on the God who's in control of everything. Think about it: in prayer, we're literally shifting our wonder. Instead of being weighed down by what we can't resolve or figure out, we're reminded that God is sovereign. He's been faithful before, and He's not about to fail us now. And let's be honest—those moments of raw prayer are often the moments we remember we're not alone, no matter how tough things get. Romans 8:28 rings true here: God is working everything, even the hard things, together for our good.

Prayer is also incredibly therapeutic, serving as a space where we can release emotions and burdens, connecting us to God for comfort and strength. The formula of prayer (2-way communication) allows us to process our inner struggles and find clarity, bringing peace in a way that research has shown can positively impact mental well-being. It's where we can be brutally honest with God, letting out what we've maybe bottle up otherwise.

Another key to building resilience is immersing yourself in Scripture. Let God's Word fill your mind and heart, because His promises are what truly anchor us. I'm telling you, there's power in declaring His promises over your life. Take Isaiah 41:10, for instance:

> *"So do not fear, for I am with you; do not be dismayed, for I am your God. I will strengthen you and help you; I will uphold you with my righteous right hand."*

Sometimes we just need to hear those words—saying them aloud can shift our focus from what seems impossible to the unstoppable power of God.

Looking back on my college experience, I realize that the overwhelming challenges I faced stemmed from a crucial oversight: I wasn't anchored in prayer or grounded in Scripture. My commitment to God was merely a reaction to my circumstances, a desperate attempt to elicit a response from Him despite the distance that had grown between us. I found myself focusing more on what He could do for me than on who He truly is. It wasn't until I hit rock bottom, feeling utterly drained and devoid of my own expectations, that I finally began to recognize His presence. Only then did I see that He had been working all along, weaving together grace and purpose that I had yet to understand.

Perhaps the delay you're experiencing isn't a sign of God's absence; rather, it's a divine pause—a sacred moment of waiting for that final piece of what's within us to be refined. Picture this:

had I received my blessing while still trapped in a cycle of reckless spending and carelessness, I would have squandered it once more. This would have only reinforced the false belief that Jesus is nothing more than a genie, here to grant wishes, rather than my true provider.

So, could it be, friend, that this obstacle you're facing isn't the real problem at all? Instead, it's a powerful tool, meticulously designed to work through the issues at hand, transforming you for the better. Instead of shying away, lean into this moment; it may just be the spark that ignites your growth and restoration.

Refined by Fire: The Goldsmith's Process of Purity

Picture this: a goldsmith stands before a fiery furnace, ready to embark on the ancient art of refining gold. He takes a clump of raw gold, heavy with impurities, and places it into a crucible. As the flames dance around it, the heat begins to rise; can you hear the gold's silent protest? If this gold could speak, it might cry out, "Isn't there an easier way? Can't we just skip this whole discomfort thing?" But that's the beauty of the process—it's the heat that reveals the truth.

As the temperature climbs, the impurities within the gold start to bubble and rise to the surface. Like hidden anxieties and uncertainties rising in our own lives when we're thrust into the pressure of fire. The goldsmith, with steady hands and a trained eye, employs a special tool to skim off the dross—those unsightly impurities that tarnish the gold's brilliance. And here's the kicker: this isn't a one-and-done deal.

The goldsmith must repeat this painstaking process, time and time again, until he achieves that stunning state of purity. It takes immense patience and dedication, but the end result? A radiant, lustrous gold that shines like nothing else, free from everything that once marred its beauty.

Now, let's draw the parallel. Just as the goldsmith uses fire to transform raw gold, God often employs the trials and tribulations of life as divine tools for our own refinement. The "heat" we experience can feel unbearable at times, but it serves a purpose—it exposes the doubts, fears, and weaknesses hiding within us. In those moments of overwhelming pressure, when it feels like we're teetering on the edge, it's essential to remember that God is diligently at work, purging us of the impurities that threaten our true value and diminish our worth. He's addressing the flaws that hinder our character from thriving in the spaces our gifts have created.

Through prayer, unwavering faith, and relentless perseverance, we become more aligned with the pure, unblemished reflection of His character that He designed us to be. The refining process is not without its challenges; it can feel grueling and relentless. But ultimately, it is through this crucible of life that we emerge as vessels of His glory, shining bright in a world desperate for light. So, embrace the heat! It's a testament to the transformation taking place within you, sculpting you into something beautiful and divine.

I could share countless stories of disappointments, setbacks, tragedies and even spiritual abuse, but overall what I have learned is that all things truly work together for good.

My dearest reader, consider this, without that setback, your tenacity would be but a whisper. Without that heartbreak, your capacity for thoughtfulness and compassion would remain untapped. And without that experience of spiritual abuse, my own journey would lack the depth of empathy that shapes my leadership today. So, gaze upon your obstacle and invite God into the conversation. Ask Him, "What is this challenge working out of me, and what new strength or wisdom are You depositing within me?" Embrace the power of these divine moments, for they are shaping you into the person you were always meant to be and removing the contamination this life has deposited.

Deep Water Moment

As you navigate the tumultuous waters of life, facing obstacles and setbacks, pause for a moment to reflect on a profoundly unsettling question: what if Peter had given up? What if he had let his weariness dictate his actions in that critical moment? The ramifications are staggering. He would never have morphed into a fisher of men, he wouldn't have embraced his role as a disciple, and he would not have stood in the Upper Room at Pentecost.

Much of what we know as the foundation of the church might have crumbled without his perseverance and obedience.

So, when the odds appear stacked against you and the night feels interminable and fruitless, will you trust in Jesus' command to try again? Will you muster the strength to push beyond yourself, holding fast to the truth that God's timing is impeccable, that His ways soar above our understanding, and that His plans for you are fashioned with goodness? Expand you net into the depths, and prepare yourself to witness the miracles and blessings God has waiting for you on the other side of your obedience. This is where transformation begins, and where your greatest breakthroughs await.

Netting New Insights

Practical Steps for Overcoming Obstacles

1. Pray for Strength and Guidance

Begin by seeking God in prayer, asking for His strength to face the challenges before you and for wisdom to navigate through them. During this prayer time, take time to listen for instruction from the Lord. (James 1:5)

2. Renew Your Mind with God's Word

Meditate on Scriptures that speak to your situation, allowing God's truth to transform your thinking and renew your perspective. Recite these scriptures throughout the day to keep God's word in your spirit. Also, pray the scriptures over yourself and your situation. (Romans 12:2)

3. Take Small, Consistent Steps Forward

Break down the obstacle into manageable steps and take consistent action, trusting that God will guide your path. (Proverbs 16:9)

4. Surround Yourself with Supportive Community

Lean on a community of faith for encouragement, prayer, and accountability as you work through your challenges. This is a good time to seek Godly counsel for support and wisdom.
(Ecclesiastes 4:9-10)

It is dangerous to fall into a pity party with people who cannot help and also do not offer any positive, biblically grounded solutions.

5. Practice Gratitude

In a world where we are constantly pursuing the next, aim to cultivate a heart of gratitude. The most important time to sit in a posture of gratitude is in the midst of difficult circumstances, by recognizing and giving thanks for God's blessings.
(1 Thessalonians 5:18)

CHAPTER 8

Deepening Your Spiritual Connection

"We must meet God in the morning and spend time with Him in the secret place if we are to grow spiritually."
– A.W. Tozer

As Believers, there comes a moment—like the plot twist in your favorite movie—where we have to wade beyond those shallow, surface-level interactions with God and plunge into the exhilarating depths of spiritual intimacy. I mean, who doesn't want to trade in a quick prayer for a deep conversation with the Creator of the cosmos? As Christians, we're not just here for one hour of Sunday morning lip service; we're called to dive headfirst into the deep end!

By now, I know you've memorized this scripture but let's view Jeremiah 33:3 once more.

> *"Call to me and I will answer you and tell you great and unsearchable things you do not know."*

Think about it: just as the disciples experienced remarkable growth in their faith by walking hand-in-hand with Jesus, we too are invited to cultivate a relationship with God that penetrates every nook and cranny of our lives. It's like upgrading from a kiddie pool to a full-blown water park adventure! So, grab your floaties suga' and let's take the plunge into the deep waters of God's love and wisdom. Trust me, there's a whole ocean of joy and revelation waiting to be explored if you're brave enough to swim out just a little further!

You see, deepening your spiritual connection begins with a desire to know God more intimately. It's not about checking off a list of religious duties but about pursuing a vibrant, life-giving relationship with the King of Kings. The disciples' lives were forever changed because they *chose* to walk with Jesus *daily*. They listened to His teachings, witnessed His miracles, and asked Him questions everyday. They weren't content with a distant knowledge of Him; they wanted to know Him personally and deeply. They didn't always get it right neither did they always understand but they consistently pursued.

In the same way, God draws us into a closer relationship with Him. In James 4:8, we are told,

"Draw near to God, and He will draw near to you."

This verse is both an invitation and a promise. The more we seek Him, the more He reveals Himself to us, deepening our understanding of His character, His love, and His plans for our lives.

The Disciples' Deepened Faith Through Their Experiences with Jesus

Luke 5 is just the beginning of how the disciples' faith deepened through their experiences with Jesus. When Peter, James, and John first met Jesus, they recognized Him as a remarkable teacher and were intrigued by His authority. But it wasn't until they followed His command to cast their nets into the deep waters that they experienced His power in a personal, tangible way. That moment of obedience led to not only filled nets but also filled hearts with awe and reverence for Jesus.

This experience drastically changed the disciples' viewpoint of who Jesus was. He wasn't just a Rabbi; He was the Son of God, capable of working wonders beyond their imagination. Their faith was no longer based on hearsay, secondhand stories or ancient scrolls; it was rooted in personal encounters with the divine. As their faith grew, so did their commitment to following Him, even when it meant leaving behind everything they knew. This exchange, caused them to leave their occupation, families and stability to follow Him. A life on the open road, filled with uncertainty, but with the Son of God.

Likewise, our faith deepens when we have personal encounters with God—moments when we see His hand at work in our lives, when we experience His presence in a tangible way, or when He answers our prayers with unexpected outcomes. These experiences remind us that God is real, that He is involved in the details of our lives, and that He is worthy of our trust and devotion.

I remember a season in my life when I was so intrigued by the story of Enoch in Genesis 5. The scriptures speak of him in a matter of 4 verses but one stood out the most to me.

> *"Enoch walked with God, and he was no longer here, for God took him." Genesis 5:24*

I constantly wondered what kind of relationship Enoch and God had to have that impressed God to the degree to take Enoch from the earth, bypassing death. I was in pursuit of that type of relationship, where being separated is unbearable. I know many theologians have the eschatological answer but the question still remains. How did Enoch's connection with the Lord influence this decision? I thrusted myself into spending more time with God. I was blown away that this was even an option, to be just taken to be with the Lord.

I found myself hungry no longer for the answer of Enoch but for God's presence. A sporadic hour of prayer turned into prolonged times of prayer, not filled with prayer requests but simply spending time. Desperate for every moment to be in His presence. To lay before Him and just be with Him. I had all the dreams and all the promises God had given me but I no longer wanted any of it; I just wanted Him.

Not fame, not popularity, not even to be understood; just Him. I know it seems odd especially in a Christian culture, where we seek God for 30 minutes before performing, so we can experience manifestations of what we've labeled as the anointing. No chains being broken, no deliverance or even remnants of bible results in our gatherings but as long as we have a good shout, we feel good; then it must be the anointing. In our culture today, we only read our bibles before we preach and stay within the pages of what's comfortable and palatable for the audience. Where our relationship is only expressed in the latest Christian song and our emotions have become our indicator of His presence because we are simply unfamiliar. Where we fiend for lights, smoke machines and big crowds; Youtube prophets and New Age parlor tricks. Our desire for God's presence has waned. The Bible speaks of our church age directly:

"For the time will come when they will not endure sound doctrine; but having itching ears, they shall heap to themselves teachers in accordance with their own lusts".
2 Timothy 4:3

We don't have time to wait on Him to inhabit the space so we give way to performance and entertainment instead of waiting. The idea of spending time with God simply because I get the opportunity to spend time with the Creator of the Universe is mundane in a microwave, prophetic witchcraft, itching ear generation. But prayer and seeking the face of God should not be done for what we can get from Him but rather, of what we have the privilege to do.

The same way, we would be ecstatic to meet the President, high-ranking official or even a celebrity these days; what about the honor that God desires to be with me. Imagine, right now, you could put this book down and simply choose to walk before the throne of the King of Kings without warning, without an appointment and just be with Him. The beauty is, He's actually expecting you! What an honor. What an invitation!

The disciples were not aware that they would be able to do what Jesus could do. They were simply honored that He called them and allowed them to be with Him. Turns out, being with Him, resulted in being able to do significant things but that never became their motivation. Relationship with God is always most important. The signs, wonders and miracles were a byproduct of their relationship.

Spiritual Disciplines that Deepen Relationship

To cultivate this deepened connection with God, we must be intentional about the formation of our spiritual disciplines. Just as the disciples spent time with Jesus daily, we too must prioritize our time with God. Here are some daily practices that can help you grow spiritually and strengthen your relationship with Him:

PRAYER AS A LIFELINE

Throughout this book, I've shared countless insights on the power of prayer, but let me be clear: its significance cannot be overstated. Prayer is not merely a spiritual discipline; it's our vital connection to God. In those moments of prayer, we lay bare our hearts, voice our struggles, and seek His wisdom. We need to move beyond treating prayer as a sheer ritual and envelop it as a profound chance to present our most authentic selves—vulnerable and real—each time we come before Him.

Philippians 4:6-7 reminds us to take everything to God in prayer, assuring us that His peace will safeguard our hearts and minds. Make it a practice to begin and end your day with prayer; let it become the bedrock of your relationship with God. Remember, it's not about how long you pray; it's about the intention behind it. I believe God would much prefer five minutes of sincere, uninterrupted quality time to five hours of distracted, disengaged "prayer" that misses the mark. So, let's commit to showing up, even if just for a few minutes, because that's where the beauty truly begins.

MEDITATION ON SCRIPTURE

The Bible is a treasure assortment of wisdom, comfort, and advice. Psalm 1:2-3 speaks of the blessings that come to those who delight in the law of the Lord and meditate on it day and night. The psalmist David wisely spoke of hiding the Word in our hearts, and I wholeheartedly agree—this practice is essential. But let's dive deeper into this truth: it's not just about keeping scripture close to avoid sin; it's also about safeguarding our hearts.

Think about it: that heart of yours, the one beating steadily in your chest right now, has a tendency to wander. Without the transformative power of God's Word penetrating it, that heart can lead you down paths of wickedness and deception. It can entice you into a journey, tempting you to advertise a price you're not truly prepared to pay—emotionally, spiritually, or even physically.

The stakes are high, my friends! When our hearts are unguarded and unanchored in scripture, they can become breeding grounds for confusion and chaos. We risk becoming prey to our own desires and lusts, chasing after fleeting pleasures that ultimately leave us empty and longing for more.

But when we fill our hearts with the life-giving Word of God, we equip ourselves with the strength and wisdom to navigate the treacherous waters of life. We can stand firm against temptation, ready to discern what is truly worth pursuing and what is merely an illusion of the fruits of this flesh. So let's commit to regularly hiding His Word deep within us—not just as a shield against sin, but as a fortress protecting our hearts from the perilous traps that lie ahead.

WORSHIP AS AN EXPRESSION OF LOVE

As we reflect on the importance of hiding God's Word in our hearts and guarding ourselves against the temptations that can lead us astray, we must also consider another vital aspect of our spiritual journey: worship.

Worship transcends mere melody and lyrics; it's a profound expression of our love and reverence for God. It's not confined to the walls of a church or the notes of a song—it's laced into the existence of our daily lives. Whether through heartfelt music, fervent prayer, or selfless acts of service, worship allows us to focus our hearts on God and recognize His unfathomable greatness.

Make worship a daily practice, my friend. Let it flow from your heart in various forms: listen to worship music that stirs your soul, sing praises that lift your spirit, or simply pause to thank God for His relentless goodness. As you cultivate this expression of love day in and day out, it transforms from a momentary act into a perpetual posture of obedience. Your lifestyle, character, and very presence will become a living testament of worship, glorifying God in everything you do.

JOURNALING YOUR SPIRITUAL JOURNEY

Journaling is a powerful tool for reflection and spiritual growth. By writing down your prayers, insights from Scripture, and/or experiences with God, you create a record of your spiritual journey. This practice can help you see patterns in how God is working in your life, speaks to you and even serve as a reminder of His faithfulness during challenging times. When I go back to past journals, I'm always encouraged at how and what God said before He showed up and also how I missed it.

FASTING FOR SPIRITUAL CLARITY

Fasting is like hitting the spiritual reset button—a biblical practice that invites us to temporarily give up our beloved crutches, like food, so we can hone in on what really matters: our relationship with God.

Jesus, in Matthew 6:16-18, lays down the law on fasting, reminding us that it's a deeply personal act, not something to flaunt like a badge of honor. Never intended to be our excuse to be antisocial or even a badge of condemnation to others. After all, nobody wants to be that person at the buffet declaring, "I'm fasting for the Lord!" Isaiah 58 spills the tea on the influential effects of fasting, illustrating how it positions us to experience God's plans in full bloom.

Think of fasting as your spiritual power-up. It doesn't twist God's arm to get Him to move; rather, it clears away the distractions so we can see what He's already set in motion. So, why not make fasting a part of your spiritual toolkit? It's a great way to seek divine guidance and deepen that ever-important reliance on Him.

As you deepen this connection, hold onto your hats—because your life is about to get a serious makeover! Your faith will bulk up, your trust in God will stand firm like a rock, and your ability to tune in to His voice will sharpen like a sharply wielded blade.

Just like those disciples expanding their nets into the deep waters, you'll tap into the abundant life God has for you—not just in the jaw-dropping miracles, but also in the everyday moments where His presence shines and His love wraps around you like a warm blanket. As you chase after Him with all your heart, may you discover that He's more than enough to quench your deepest thirsts and guide you through every twist and turn life throws your way.

Deep Water Moment

As we travel through the incredible stories of scripture, we find a powerful reminder echoing through the ages: we are called to dive deeper into our spiritual lives. Just as the disciples were compelled to leave the comfort of the shore and plunge into the deep waters to experience something more, so too are we invited to break free from the shallows of a superficial faith and mediocre religion. This is your Deep Water Moment—a divine summons to pursue God with an insatiable passion, to seek Him with every fiber of your being, and to entrust Him with every facet of your existence.

Pause for a moment and reflect: How can I deepen my relationship with God? What bold steps can I take today to draw closer to Him? Let these questions wash over you like waves, and remember the profound promise found in James 4:8:

"Draw near to God, and He will draw near to you."

He stands at the edge of the deep, eagerly awaiting your leap of faith, ready to unveil the depths of His love and wisdom. Embrace this adventure; let the currents of His grace sweep you into a journey of self-discovery filled with profound spiritual growth. The depths await, and within them lies a connection with God that will change everything. Are you ready to dive in? Hold your breath...Jump!

Netting New Insights

Practical Steps for Deepening Your Spiritual Connection

1. Set a Daily Prayer Schedule

Establish a consistent time each day for prayer. Whether it's early in the morning or before bed, make prayer a non-negotiable part of your day.

2. Engage in Regular Bible Study

Don't just read the Bible—study it. Use study guides, commentaries, or join a Bible study group to dive deeper into God's Word.

3. Create a Worship Playlist

Curate a playlist of worship songs that resonate with your spirit. Let this music fill your home, your car, or your workspace, creating an atmosphere of worship wherever you go.

4. Keep a Prayer Journal

As you pray, begin to write the song, scripture or even the prayer that comes to your heart. Also capture what God said during your time. If that feels too taxing, feel free to start with something a little lighter:

Each day, write down three things you are grateful for. This practice shifts your focus from what you lack to what God has already provided, fostering a heart of worship and thanksgiving.

5. Fast Regularly

Choose a rhythm to incorporate fasting into your lifestyle. During this fasting time, be sure to dedicate that time to prayer and seeking God's direction in your life. While you can fast from several things, the Bible only speaks to fasting as abstaining from food and beverages either absolute, liquid only and Daniel Fast. You are welcome to include social media, entertainment, music genres, etc.

CHAPTER 9

Expand Your Net

"Life's most persistent and urgent question is, 'What are you doing for others?'"
– Martin Luther King, Jr.

As we jump into personal growth and spiritual depth, it's essential to recognize that our transformation extends far beyond our own lives; it has the potential to create a ripple effect in the world around us. In our focal scriptural text, the miracle of surplus served not as a mere spectacle but as a catalyst for a much grander calling. The reflection you see in the mirror today is just the beginning of the greatness God has in store for you.

Let's be clear, Jesus didn't perform this phenomenon simply to astound anyone. He was equipping Peter and the other disciples to expand their nets wider and reach beyond their current limitations. Just as Peter's obedience led to a bountiful catch, our willingness to embrace our divinely appointed purpose can yield profound impacts on those around us.

At that pivotal moment in Luke 5, Peter could hardly envision the significance of what was unfolding; he was focused solely on his immediate circumstances; all the things that stood in his way. Yet, what seemed trivial at the time was crucial in the spiritual realm, setting the course for a life of extraordinary impact.

Our gifts and purpose are designed to serve others and glorify God. In reality, you are not the problem but rather a solution to one, remember? Once we are able to step out of our insecurities and move past our own shortcomings, we can begin to see that God truly knows what He's doing in us. When you step into your role, embracing the full vision of who God created you to be, a ripple effect that extends far beyond yourself and our immediate circles is created. You are the stone that cascades ripples into the pond of your life but also the lives connected and affected by your existence.

The early disciples, many once ordinary fishermen, became powerful witnesses of Christ's resurrection and bearers of His message. Their ministry, fueled by their deepened faith and newfound purpose, transformed communities and spread the Gospel across nations. This ripple effect is a testament to the potential impact each of us can have when we fully embrace and utilize our gifts.

The Ripple Effect

After Jesus' ascension, the disciples were empowered to expand their nets beyond the shores of Galilee. Can you imagine these "nobodies" realizing that Jesus had not only called them to follow but He was equipping them for something beyond themselves all the time? Something truly beyond this world. They went on to establish the early church, performing miracles, preaching the Gospel, and spreading the message of Jesus Christ.

Their lives are a living testament to the power of embracing God's call and the ripple effect it can have. The growth of the early church and the spread of Christianity across the globe are direct results of the disciples' obedience to Jesus' command and their willingness to step into that boat one more time. Friend, what is it that God has deposited into you that is beyond where you are right now?

As we continue to reflect on this incredible journey, it's clear that the disciples' obedience and faith didn't just change their own lives—it transformed the world around them. They moved from a place of ordinary tasks to one of extraordinary impact, driven by the power and purpose Jesus instilled in them. The ripple effect of their ministry continues to be felt across generations, proving that when we respond to God's call, our influence can extend far beyond our immediate surroundings and our imagination.

This brings us to the true meaning of "Expand Your Net." Just as the disciples were called to stretch beyond their familiar roles and embrace a higher purpose, we too are invited to expand our reach. It's about realizing that what God has placed within us is meant to touch lives, to foster growth, and to create a legacy of faith that echoes beyond time. Expanding your net is not just about personal growth and spiritual transformation—it's about allowing God to use you in ways that impact others and advance His kingdom.

It's Time to Launch Out

Get ready to dive headfirst into the exhilarating depths of faith and purpose! We've been on quite the adventure, peeling back the layers of what it truly means to *Expand Your Net.* This isn't just a catchy phrase—it's a resounding call to live with intention, audacity, and an unwavering commitment to God's grand design for YOU.

Expanding your net is a clarion call to step boldly into the unknown, to embrace the unique purpose that God has crafted specifically for you. It's a powerful declaration that transcends limitations and dares you to live life fully, impacting everyone around you. This journey invites you to rise above self-doubt and fear, as you cultivate growth and transformation in every aspect of your life. With each act of faith, you broaden your horizons and deepen your influence, becoming a beacon of hope and inspiration to those you encounter. Let this mantra resonate within you: I will expand my net, stepping into my divine purpose, impacting the world, and growing beyond all barriers. This is not just a call to action; it's a promise of the extraordinary life God has waiting for you.

So, let's kick fear and doubt to the curb, shall we? It's time to launch out with courage, expanding your reach and influence for His glory. The Kingdom of God needs your influence, your voice, your gift for such a time as this. The world is waiting for you to make waves—water feels great—c'mon in!

Stepping Out in Faith

Nestled in the flow of who God says you are is refreshing, fulfilling, and charged with possibilities. Just as you feel the urge to plunge deeper into those refreshing waters, expanding your net means diving headfirst into the unknown with God guiding your every stroke.

This isn't just a casual swim friend; it requires a willingness to engage in what I like to call "extreme obedience." This is where your faith meets action, where you challenge yourself to not just believe in God's promises but to put those beliefs into motion, even when you're navigating through foggy uncertainty. Sure, it's easier to trust when the path is laid out in front of you like a well-marked trail. But much like relying on your car's navigation system—blindly trusting it to lead you through the twists, turns and detours toward your destination—you must also have faith that God knows where you're headed and has mapped out the best route to get there.

When that navigation voice instructs you to turn right, you might falter, wondering if it's the right move. But you push past your hesitation and follow the directions regardless. That's exactly how we need to operate in our walk of faith. For me, extreme obedience meant acting on God's promptings even when I was left in the dark about the details or even the next steps. If you know me at all, you know I thrive on details; a lack of them can send my mind into a tailspin! And trust me, God knows this about me too.

I still remember the moment God first whispered the phrase "extreme obedience" into my spirit during a time of prayer and consecration. It felt profound and thrilling, but honestly, I had no idea what it truly meant at that time. Little did I know, He was about to unfold this concept in the most unexpected and life-changing ways.

A few days after that moment, I had an inner vision. This may be a new term for some so let me elaborate a bit here. An "inner vision" refers to a mental image or insight that arises from deep within a person, often during moments of contemplation, prayer, or meditation. It's like seeing a vivid picture or scenario in your mind's eye (the place where you daydream) that conveys a message, idea, or feeling.

There I was standing in a room surrounded by boxes—each one filled with bottles of oil. The vision was so vivid, and then I heard God's voice: "You need to get bottles." My first reaction was disbelief. I was already feeling overwhelmed by the obligations of life, stretched to my limits keeping up with God's plans, and now He wants me to get bottles for oil? My mind raced with doubt and reservation. "I must have misheard," I thought to myself. But God's response was swift and clear: "Obedience doesn't require understanding; it requires following instructions."

This was my moment of truth. I had pledged myself to the concept of extreme obedience in prayer, but now I stood at a crossroads. Would I honor my commitment and say "yes" even when the path ahead was shrouded in uncertainty? I felt a flicker of hesitation, yet before I knew it, I found myself scouring the internet for bottles, completely oblivious to the purpose behind this quest or what it all signified.

When those clear Boston bottles with black screw caps landed on my doorstep, I stood there like a deer in headlights, feeling equal parts confused and intrigued. "Now what on Earth am I supposed to do with these?" Just then, a familiar voice echoed in my spirit: "You're going to make the oil. Find the recipe in Scripture."

At that moment, my heart took a nosedive to my feet. "Wait, what?! Make oil? Who, me? I didn't even know normal people could make oil, let alone that there were recipes tucked away in the

Bible to use today? Is this some divine cooking show I accidentally signed up for?"

I couldn't help but chuckle at the absurdity of it all, while my mind raced with visions of me fumbling through the kitchen, looking for the "Holy Grail" of oil-making. Little did I know, this was the start of a wild adventure that would blend the sacred with the mundane in ways I had never imagined!

As I searched for where God wanted me to start, there it was, the first recipe in Exodus 30, plain as day. I realized then that this wasn't just a test of my obedience; it was a test of my willingness to follow God's instructions, even when they made no sense to me, especially without details.

I learned that extreme obedience isn't about having all the answers or even understanding the why behind God's commands. It's about surrendering to His voice, trusting that His plans are perfect, and moving forward, even when the path is unclear. It's about letting go of our need to comprehend and simply saying, "Yes, Lord, I will follow."

> *"Faith is the substance of things hoped for, the evidence of things not seen." Hebrews 11:1*

This verse encourages us to act on the belief that God's plans for us are good, even when we cannot see the full picture. When the disciples obeyed Jesus and let down their nets in deep waters, their faith was rewarded abundantly, demonstrating that obedience to

God's word opens the door to divine provision. Similarly, Proverbs 3:5-6 urges us to

> *"Trust in the Lord with all your heart and lean not on your own understanding; in all your ways submit to him, and he will make your paths straight."*

This passage highlights the vital necessity of placing our trust in God's wisdom rather than our own, particularly when He beckons us to take bold steps of faith.

To expand your net means living in the assurance that God's guidance will usher you into a realm of blessings, fulfillment, and purpose. It involves relinquishing your fears and doubts, taking that daring leap of faith, and believing that your obedience will cultivate a greater harvest in your life—one that may be hidden from your view but is already waiting, crafted by God's unchanging hand.

Embracing Your God-Given Purpose

Fully owning the unique identity and purpose God has crafted for you is a part of expanding your net. It involves not only recognizing the gifts and talents He has placed within you but also actively nurturing them and curating an environment for optimal growth. This means investing time in developing your skills and exploring various methods, as these traits are not random—they are deliberately given to help you fulfill your God-given calling.

To grasp this truth, you must shift your perspective. See yourself through God's eyes, where you are valued and equipped for greatness, rather than through the lens of self-doubt or past limitations. Remember, you are not an accident; you were designed intentionally with a purpose that fits into God's master plan. Your gifts are not solely for your own satisfaction; they are meant to create a positive impact on the world around you.

Again, the Bible affirms this in Ephesians 2:10:

> *"For we are God's masterpiece. He has created us anew in Christ Jesus, so we can do the good things he planned for us long ago."*

You are God's workmanship, created with care and intention. This verse highlights that your purpose is not something you need to strive to create, but rather something you are to discover and walk in, as God has already prepared it for you.

When you wholeheartedly embrace the person God created you to be, you unleash the dynamite power of the Holy Spirit within you, shattering the chains of insecurity and fear that have held you captive for far too long. As you cultivate the unique gifts He has bestowed upon you, you align yourself with His purpose, stretching your net to capture opportunities beyond your wildest dreams. This is where true fulfillment is found—living in the abundant truth of who God says you are and stepping fearlessly into the exceptional destiny He has already prepared just for you.

As you pursue this path, you'll discover that while the world may seem overcrowded and saturated with voices, the lane that God has carved out for you is wide open, eagerly awaiting your arrival. It's a space designated exclusively for you, where only you can shine and create significant, lasting Kingdom impact. So step into it! Walk in your calling with confidence, knowing that your place is not just a possibility; it is a promise waiting to be fulfilled!

Impacting Others

Expanding your net shatters the notion of personal success only; it is a heavenly call to reimagine your reach and bless those around you. Just as the disciples found their nets overflowing—not just for their own benefit but to nourish and uplift many—your growth is meant to create waves of change that resonate through the lives of others around you. Remember the ripple effect?

This road of discovering and cultivating your purpose is not solely about you; it's about the multitude of hearts that will be stirred, encouraged, and uplifted through your faithful response to God's calling. And they extend far beyond the confines of a church building. They can be found within your family dynamics, the challenges of governmental systems, the chaos of social media, the bustling marketplace—anywhere you look; God has curated moments and opportunities untainted and waiting just for you.

I know, I feel your spirit– the prospect of making such a profound impact can feel daunting. The shadow of self-doubt looms large, whispering fears of inadequacy, mistakes, and the burden of responsibility, even now. You might find yourself questioning, "Who am I to make a difference? How dare you? What if I stumble?" These feelings are valid, friend, but they must be countered with the unwavering truth of God's word, reminding you that your obedience can ignite revival far beyond your own understanding and idiosyncrasies.

I write to you today as a testimony to a new season in my own life—one where fear and doubt no longer grip my heart with iron fists. But let me be real: this hasn't always been my story. The road to freedom has felt like a relentless uphill climb, one that I still battle daily to keep from slipping back into the shadows. Like so many of us in this faith journey, I've wrestled with doubt. But for me, it wasn't a question of God's ability or His willingness to act; it was a darker, more cunning doubt—a whisper in my ear that questioned my worth. The haunting thought wasn't, "Can He do it?" but rather, "Do I have what it takes to meet His expectations and see this through?"

I know that feeling, that quiet voice that looms over your aspirations, as you wonder if you're enough to fulfill the calling you feel stirring deep within. You're not alone in this struggle, and I want you to know that the path to believing in your worth is a journey worth taking.

For years, the enemy had a field day with my mind, planting whispers that I naively accepted as my own thoughts. After moments of preaching, teaching, or being powerfully used by God, those insidious voices would slink in, murmuring, "Was that good enough? What if He still says, 'I don't know you,' like in the scriptures? Was that even God or just you pretending?"

Those doubts would pull me into a dark pit, snatching away the joy and celebration of what God was doing through me and the fact that I was walking through answered prayers. I found myself wrestling with these feelings, torn between whether they were just my natural insecurities or something more sinister. I prayed fervently, seeking clarity and strength, constantly battling the weight of condemnation that suggested I, an insecure person, was somehow unworthy of God's use.

In my prayers, I initially mistook these feelings for humility. I thought it was proper to feel small in the face of God's great work. But the truth was, I was allowing the enemy and myself to diminish what God was doing by convincing me that I wasn't enough. I didn't realize the toll this took on my mind—it triggered nervousness, anxiety, and a constant sense of inadequacy that spread to other areas of my life. Despite the visions, the prophecies, the signs, and the testimonies, I couldn't shake the lie that I wasn't capable of making the impact God created me for. It was too big and I simply wasn't enough. The enemy had me convinced that, despite everything, I wasn't good enough to be used in such a powerful way.

Then, like a sound from Heaven, God began to reveal the truth to me found in 2 Timothy 1:7,

> *"For God has not given us a spirit of fear, but of power and of love and of a sound mind."*

This verse struck a chord in my heart, reassuring me that God had already equipped me with everything I needed to fulfill His purpose. He'd already given power, love and a sound mind. The courage to step into the influence He entrusted to me was already within me—I just had to embrace it.

Now, let me speak this powerful truth into your life: you are precisely who God has designed you to be. The gifts, talents, and purpose He has weaved into your very being are monumental. You are a city on a hill, shining brightly for all to see (Matthew 5:14). Hiding is simply not an option. God is ready to use you to create a significant impact in your sphere of influence, and the privilege of that influence is one of the greatest honors He can grant. Embrace this calling with confidence, for you are already enough in His eyes.

This Holy Spirit authority signifies that God entrusts you with the hearts and lives of others, believing that through you, His love and truth can flow. Don't take this trust lightly, but don't let it intimidate you either. God doesn't demand perfection; He only seeks your willingness to be a vessel poured out for His purpose.

As you expand your net by mentoring, supporting, and inspiring those around you, you become an instrument of His grace, guiding others to discover and step into their own God-given destiny. Let people see you, truly see the authentic you and what God can do with even you.

Look again at the disciples—ordinary fishermen, tax collectors, and zealots—whom Jesus entrusted with a world-changing message. Their impact stemmed not from lofty qualifications but from their simple willingness to follow Him and share what they received. Likewise, your ability to make a difference isn't defined by your credentials but by your openness to be used by God to reach and transform others for Him. As you wrap your mind around this honored privilege, you'll find that the more you pour out, the more God fills your net—not just for your benefit, but for all those He has called you to bless.

Living Beyond Limitations

I know, I know, at this point you might need a break from the overall concept of expanding your net. Friend, the reality is that this is a bold call to rise above the chains of past failures, fears, and doubts that have held you back. It's an invitation from the Father to finally break free from the small, safe spaces you've confined yourself to and to step into the vast, boundless potential He has placed within you. Expanding your net isn't just about doing more; it's about becoming more—more of who God created you to be.

So often, we allow our past mistakes or the fear of the unknown to dictate our future. To stifle our trajectory. We underestimate ourselves, convinced that we're not enough, that our dreams are too big, or that God's plans are too grandiose for someone like us. But expanding your net is challenging all the limitations and embracing the truth of who you are in Christ. Recognizing that you are fearfully and wonderfully made (Psalm 139:14), and that God's vision for your life is far more expansive and beautiful than you could ever imagine.

My dearest reader, God doesn't see you through the lens of your past failures; He sees you through the lens of His love and purpose. He calls you, to dream bigger, to believe in the remarkable plans He has for you. Jeremiah 29:11 reminds us,

> *"For I know the plans I have for you," declares the Lord, "plans to prosper you and not to harm you, plans to give you hope and a future."*

This is a call to trust that God's plans for you are not only good but are also grand and life-changing. This vision requires a deep shift in perspective—a willingness to see yourself as God sees you: capable, equipped, destined for greatness and FEARLESS. It's about believing that you are more than your past, more than your fears, and more than the doubts that try to keep you diminutive. When you expand your net, you'll step into a life that is aligned with God's purpose, and you will begin to live out the extraordinary story He has written for you.

Continuously Growing

Expanding your net isn't just about one big moment of stepping out in faith—it's about a lifelong commitment to growth. It means that your spiritual, mental, and emotional development is ongoing, constantly being refined and stretched by God. Just as a fisherman continually adjusts and expands his nets to catch more fish, you are called to continually expand your heart, mind, and spirit to align more with God's will and to make a greater impact in the world.

Investing in your expansion and growth is one of the most powerful decisions you can make in your journey of faith and purpose. This commitment means actively pursuing opportunities that stretch your abilities and deepen your understanding, enabling you to become the person God has called you to be.

This investment could take many forms, such as continuing your education to gain new skills or knowledge in areas that align with your purpose. Whether it's taking a course in leadership, enrolling in a Bible program, or even going back to school, education is a key tool in expanding your net.

It might also involve seeking therapy or counseling to address and heal from past wounds, allowing you to move forward unburdened by old fears and doubts. Therapy can help you gain emotional clarity and resilience, equipping you to handle the challenges that come with growth.

Additionally, investing in spiritual mentorship can provide guidance and accountability as you navigate new levels of faith and purpose. Surrounding yourself with a community of like-minded individuals who are also committed to growth can create a support system that encourages you to keep pushing forward.

Ultimately, investing in your growth means being proactive in seeking out the resources. Truth is, this growth happens through your openness to new experiences and your willingness to learn from every situation, whether it's a success or a failure. Each challenge becomes an opportunity for God to stretch your faith and increase your capacity. As you grow spiritually, you become more aware of the vastness of God's calling on your life and realize that your journey with Him is never static. Philippians 1:6 reminds us,

"Being confident of this, that He who began a good work in you will carry it on to completion until the day of Christ Jesus."

Listen, embracing ongoing growth means acknowledging that your journey doesn't end at a particular milestone or victory. Instead, there is always a deeper level of understanding to gain, a higher level of faith to attain, and new opportunities to glorify God with your life. Expanding your net means not becoming complacent, but continuing to press forward, allowing God to refine and use you in even greater ways.

Your spiritual walk doesn't have a finish line: this side of heaven—there's always more to explore, more to discover about God's character, and more ways for Him to work through you. Your finish line is when your work is complete and you are received into those pearly gates, until then, onward march!

With every step you've taken so far, you've been laying the groundwork for something far greater than yourself. But before we conclude this journey, there's one more crucial step—understanding how to sustain this newfound influence and continue growing. As we move into the final chapter, prepare to tie together everything you've learned and discover how to maintain your momentum as you expand your net.

Deep Water Moment

It's essential to understand that this adventure transcends mere personal milestones or accomplishments. It solicits you to immerse yourself in the breathtaking vision God has intricately designed for your life—one that beckons you to make a meaningful impact on others in ways you might never have imagined. This realization is pivotal: you are not only called to live a life of purpose, but also to be a catalyst for change in the world around you by fully embracing the unique person God made you to be.

Yes, the challenges—doubt, fear, limitations—are very real. But remember, they pale in comparison to the greatness of the God who called you. This chapter encourages you to break free from the constraints of small thinking and to embrace the expansive vision that lies ahead. It's not about seeking glory for yourself; it's about recognizing that your life serves as an instrument in God's hands to transform communities, touch hearts, and spread His love far and wide.

So, what does this practically mean for you? It means choosing not to retreat in the face of what seems overwhelming, but rather to step boldly into the depths of what God is asking you to do. It means acting in faith, even when the waters appear daunting and the current threatens to pull you under. Your willingness to respond to God's call is the key that will not only unlock your own potential but also release the potential of those around you.

Pause for a moment and reflect on the journey you've taken thus far—how has God stretched and shaped you? In what ways have you caught glimpses of His grander vision for your life? Now is the time to challenge yourself to widen your net even further, embracing the confidence that comes from being equipped and empowered by the Holy Spirit. Your influence extends beyond your own life; it's meant for the lives that God has destined for you to touch. This is your moment to dive into the deep waters of your calling, trusting that God will not only guide and sustain you but will also use you to make a transformative difference in this world. Your journey is just beginning, and the best is yet to come.

Netting New Insights

Practical Steps for Expanding Your Net

1. Identify Your Gifts

Take time to reflect on the strengths and passions that God has placed within you. As Pastor Theo Schaffer always says, "Purpose has a pattern." You're usually not as off base as it feels. What comes naturally to you? What non-paid activities bring you joy and fulfillment? These are often indicators of the gifts God has given you. Once identified, seek to align these gifts with your purpose. Use them to serve others and bring glory to God. (1 Peter 4:10)

Example: If you have a talent for teaching, consider volunteering in a local church or community organization to assist with an instructional program.

2. Invest in Opportunities for Growth

Look for ways to celebrate and continue growing. This may be reading books on the subject, taking classes or even being mentored by someone in the area you're aspiring to be a part of or even grow in. We must always be learners.

3. Lead By Example

Your life can be a powerful testimony to others. By living out your purpose with authenticity and courage, you inspire those around you to pursue their own paths with confidence. Your actions can serve as a model for others, showing them what is possible when they trust God and step out in faith. (Matthew 5:16)

Example: If you're committed to serving your community, make it a priority to show up consistently and with enthusiasm. Your dedication will encourage others to do the same.

CHAPTER 10

Living a Life of Fulfillment

"To each there comes in their lifetime a special moment when they are figuratively tapped on the shoulder and offered the chance to do a very special thing, unique to them and fitted to their talents. What a tragedy if that moment finds them unprepared or unqualified for that which could have been their finest hour."
Winston Churchill

Riding the Waves of Purpose

As we draw nearer to the breathtaking climax of our journey together, I urge you to take a moment—a heartbeat in time—to pause, breathe, and truly absorb the gravity of this moment. Reflect on the stunning metamorphosis that has transpired within you. Remember that pivotal instant when you dared to cast your nets into the uncharted depths of your potential, when you bravely embraced your true identity and divine purpose. This quest for expansion has not been merely transformative; it has been nothing short of revolutionary.

You have weathered storms of uncertainty, confronted the monsters of your past with an unyielding courage, and deepened your spiritual connection in ways that have forever reshaped the fabric of your existence. Now, here you stand, on the precipice of a new dawn—an existence overflowing with purpose and fulfillment. Legacy beckons you, my friend.

Before we turn the page on this chapter, I feel compelled to share one last story, a raw reflection that underscores the personal nature of our walk with God. In Chapter 6, I spoke of my "come to Jesus" moment during my college years, but now I must peel back the layers to reveal the darkness that nearly consumed, even me.

Despite the growth we've celebrated, this journey is an intensely individual one. There comes a moment when you must resolutely choose to be all in with Jesus, even when the path ahead seems shrouded in shadows.

My moment of reckoning struck me unexpectedly, a jarring wake-up call while I was trapped in the suffocating grip of hypocrisy and disillusionment. I had always felt a deep connection with God—a thirst for the divine that pulsed through my veins. Yet, time and time again, my faith was tested as I watched less committed individuals—those who had strayed so far from the calling—rise to heights I could only dream of.

I saw the club-hopping choir directors, the wayward preachers, and the unenthusiastic pew warmers thriving in the very arenas I longed to inhabit. After all, I had a word from the Lord, remember. Jealousy crept in subtly, wrapping its cold fingers around my heart, making me question my resolve. Here I was, striving for holiness and righteousness while feeling utterly unrewarded.

The insidious culture of hypocrisy within the church made it all too easy to slip into complacency. It became acceptable to live a double life—to indulge in sin while maintaining the façade of faith within the four walls. I won't deceive you into thinking it was solely my church that led me astray; it was my own wavering commitment, my lack of consistent focus on Jesus that allowed me to be lulled into the very behaviors I once preached against. I was busy doing all the "right" things, completing my checklist of Christian living; yet a haze clouded my judgment and decisions, leaving me lost, confused and without connection to the Father.

Amidst this turmoil, I found myself entangled in a relationship with someone who cared little for me, only for what I could offer. I was a mere puppet in his play—chauffeuring him through life while grappling with the shame of my own choices. My heart was at war, battling between my faith and my desires, and I felt as though I were drifting further and further from the shore of my salvation. Then came the moment that shattered my already fragile world: I discovered I was pregnant. The weight of my situation crushed me; I couldn't imagine forging ahead with a child in the midst of my chaotic existence. After all, I wasn't sure if I wanted to live myself.

In a moment of despair, I made a harrowing decision to terminate the life growing within me. I justified my actions, but deep down, I was drowning in guilt and confusion. I barely remember the procedure—everything felt like a blur, as if I were merely a passenger in my own life, disconnected from the God I had once known intimately. My mind echoed with the certainty of His presence during my freshman year, now replaced by an overwhelming sense of abandonment not long after. My world was crumbling, and I was spiraling into darkness.

One fateful night, as I drove back from another reckless rendezvous, I felt myself slipping away, sleep overtaking me behind the wheel. For those who know me, this was unthinkable—I had never before lost consciousness while driving. Yet, there I was, my hands slipping from the wheel as I drifted toward an uncertain fate. In that moment of panic, I fought to awaken, but a paralyzing weight gripped my body. My eyes flew open to the horrifying sight of my car barreling down the highway at over 90 mph, my foot glued to the accelerator.

Desperation surged within me as I searched for help, my voice strangled in my throat. But then, amidst the chaos, I caught a glimpse of something extraordinary—a brilliant figure atop an optic white horse, galloping alongside me as if racing against my impending doom. I blinked, my heart racing, and the vision sharpened into focus. This luminous being, radiating a warm glow, appeared to reach out to me with his gaze, yet I remained ensnared in my own despair. Perhaps this was the intervention I needed? Perhaps this was the way my story was destined to conclude.

Suddenly, as if in answer to my silent plea, the horse struck my car, spinning it violently to a halt—my world jolting to a stop as if I had collided with an unyielding wall. Tears streamed down my cheeks as I heard the unmistakable voice of God like thunder: "I will allow you to die in your sins, if you don't take action to change." In that instant, the paralysis lifted, and I gasped for breath, realizing I was mere feet from a guardrail that would have sent me over the edge into oblivion.

On the side of that highway, I collapsed, heartbroken and repentant to God. I knew that everything had to change. I severed ties with the people and habits that had led me astray, I confessed my sins to my leadership, and I made a commitment to start anew. This story serves as a reminder that while we can outline the perfect plans and paths, the ultimate choice to be sold out for Jesus lies within you, alone.

There's no room for complacency when you're living a life of fulfillment. You must weave every thought, every action, and every decision into the vibrant tapestry of God's purpose for your existence. Everything else becomes secondary to His divine mandate. Your unique gifts and calling were not meant for solitary enjoyment; they are designed to uplift and inspire those around you for Him.

As you step into this exhilarating new chapter, take a moment to breathe, close your eyes, and absorb the weight of this pivotal juncture. Remember where your journey began—those dark days when self-doubt whispered insidiously, when shadows loomed large, and light felt like a distant memory.

Yet, against all odds, a remarkable shift occurred. The dawn broke through the darkness, illuminating the brilliance that has always resided within you. You have transformed in ways you once thought impossible, emerging stronger, wiser, and profoundly attuned to the divine potential that God embedded in your soul long before time began.

Let me share an essential truth that you must hold close: this is just the beginning. Every victory you've achieved and every breakthrough you've experienced have been stepping stones, guiding you to this critical juncture—a moment where you shift from living solely for yourself to embracing a higher purpose. Now is the time to fully step into the person you are meant to be, to continue your ascent, and to make a lasting impact on the world around you.

However, with this elevation comes a sobering reality. An adversary waits in the shadows, determined to cling to his hold as you embrace your purpose and expand your net. I mention this not to instill fear but to remind you of an undeniable truth: you were made for this! If the enemy could have derailed the divine plan that

God has for your life, he would have done so long ago. But he cannot. That doesn't mean the journey ahead will be free of challenges. Adversity will emerge, fierce and relentless. But listen closely, my friend—you were made for this! Your journey is far from over; it is just beginning, and the world is eager to witness the greatness you have yet to reveal.

Forging a New Path: Becoming a Bloodline Breaker and Establishing a Legacy of Faith

You are not just an agent of change; you are a warrior. Your influence reaches far beyond the present; it shapes the future you are crafting and the legacy you are leaving behind. You don't know it yet, but it's still true. God is using you to shatter the chains that have bound your family for generations. You are the bloodline breaker, the one chosen to forge a lineage of warriors for the Kingdom of God. The marketplace needs someone like you, and our schools are yearning for your voice. You were designed to stand firm where others have faltered, to declare, "This cycle ends with me." Whether it's breaking free from generational curses, overcoming patterns of dysfunction, or escaping spiritual stagnation, you are called to rewrite the narrative for future generations.

As a bloodline breaker, you stand in the gap, interceding and actively engaging in God's work of redemption and renewal within your family. Scripture is rich with examples of the profound effects of generational blessings and curses, as well as the transformative power of an individual's faith and obedience.

Consider **Gideon (Judges 6-8)**, who was called by God to rescue Israel from the Midianites. When God first approached him, He commanded Gideon to destroy his father's altar to Baal and the Asherah pole beside it. This bold action not only broke the hold of idolatry within his family but also set in motion the deliverance of an entire nation. Gideon's story illustrates the courage it takes to break free from destructive family patterns and establish a new spiritual legacy.

Look at **Josiah (2 Kings 22-23)**, who became a bloodline breaker by leading a revival in Judah, erasing the idolatry and wickedness of his forebears. Born into a lineage of kings who led Israel astray, Josiah chose to seek God and restore the nation's faith. His reforms were so impactful that they delayed God's judgment on Judah for a time.

And then there's **Rahab (Joshua 2, 6; Matthew 1:5)**, a Canaanite woman from a pagan culture destined for destruction. Her faith in the God of Israel prompted her to hide the Israelite spies, securing salvation for herself and her family. Rahab's courageous actions not only spared her household but also positioned her as an ancestor of Jesus Christ, breaking her family's ties to idolatry and aligning it with God's purpose.

Embracing your purpose begins with a deep and introspective journey to identify the negative patterns or curses that have lingered in your family line. These patterns may appear as spiritual struggles, such as idolatry and disobedience to God, or as personal battles like addiction and broken relationships. Just as David cried out in Psalm 139:23-24,

> *"Search me, O God, and know my heart; try me and know my thoughts! And see if there be any grievous way in me, and lead me in the way everlasting,"*

you too must invite the Holy Spirit to shine a light on the areas in your life that need transformation.

Once these patterns are uncovered, the next step is to renounce them in the name of Jesus, breaking any agreements or covenants made by previous generations. You are not bound by the mistakes of those who came before you. Remember the authority given to you in Luke 10:19, where Jesus declares,

> *"Behold, I have given you authority to tread on serpents and scorpions, and over all the power of the enemy, and nothing shall hurt you."*

This is your divine empowerment to shatter the chains of the past and walk in the freedom that Christ has secured for you.

As you break free from these patterns, it's crucial to replace them with new, Godly practices. If your family history includes broken marriages, commit to building a Christ-centered marriage. If there's been a legacy of poverty, embrace biblical principles of stewardship and generosity. Romans 12:2 encourages us to be

*"transformed by the renewal of your mind, that by testing
you may discern what is the will of God, what is good and
acceptable and perfect."*

This transformation will lay the groundwork for a new legacy for
your family. Interceding for your family is another vital part of
being a bloodline breaker. To intercede means to intervene or
mediate on behalf of another, especially in prayer. The Hebrew
word often associated with intercession is "פָּגַע" (paga), meaning
"to meet," "to encounter," or "to entreat." This term is used in the
context of intercession to describe the act of coming before God on
behalf of others.

In Isaiah 53:12, the word "paga" signifies a deep engagement in
prayer, where one "hits the mark" or makes an intense appeal to
God. This shows that intercession is not a passive act but one
requiring passion, persistence, and sometimes even confrontation
in the spiritual realm.

Stand in the gap through prayer, commanding the chains of past
generations to break and relying solely on God to bring healing
and restoration. Just as Moses interceded for Israel in Exodus
32:11-14, resulting in God relenting from His wrath, your prayers
have the potential to bring about divine intervention and change.

Lastly, share your journey. Your story of overcoming and
breakthrough can inspire others to do the same. Revelation 12:11
reminds us,

"they have conquered him by the blood of the Lamb and by the word of their testimony."

Your story is not just for you; I know it feels like it, but it's a beacon of hope for others who may be facing similar struggles. As believers, this isn't merely a responsibility; it's our duty. Let's confront the sins and struggles that have plagued our families for generations and establish a new, Godly legacy. Through the power of the Holy Spirit, you are equipped to break these chains and set a new course for future generations. Your obedience will not only transform your life but also the lives of those who follow you, paving the way for a legacy of faith, strength, and victory in the Kingdom of God. This is your divine invitation to be the change that reshapes not only your life but the lives of generations to come. The time is now; this is your moment. All of creation is waiting!

For the creation waits in eager expectation for the children of God to be revealed. Romans 8:19

It doesn't matter what came before—what matters is that you are here now. And that poses a challenge to anything that stands in your way because you are about to expand your net like never before.

So stand tall, honey! Embrace the power that resides within you. You are stepping into a calling far greater than you can imagine, and the world around you will be forever changed because of it and God is on your side.

As we conclude, I invite you to reflect once more on the profound lesson from Luke 5:4. Remember when Jesus instructed the disciples to cast their nets on the other side of the boat? This wasn't merely about catching more fish—it was a divine invitation to embrace a new vision for their lives. Today, God extends that same invitation to you. He's urging you to cast your net wide, step boldly into your influence, share your gifts generously, and create a meaningful impact on the world around you.

The promise in Exodus 33:14 reassures us,

"My Presence will go with you, and I will give you rest."

This is a reminder that you are never alone on this path. God's presence is with you, offering guidance, peace, and the strength to fulfill your purpose with unwavering confidence and grace. As you continue your journey, remember that your actions create ripples that extend far beyond yourself. Your life is a testament to the transformative power of faith and purpose.

Carry with you the lessons learned, the strength gained, and the confidence that you are exactly who God has called you to be. Continue to expand your net, breaking free from the confines of your comfort zone and embracing the full breadth of your divine calling. Your story is powerful, your purpose significant, and your impact limitless.

Deep Water Moment

As you stand at the edge of the deep waters, ready to cast your net once more, let this moment of reflection be both a pause and a launchpad. Take a deep breath and acknowledge the incredible journey you've embarked upon. The waters may seem daunting, and the path may still be unfolding, but this is your moment.

Reflect on the steps you have taken, the growth you have experienced, and the resilience you have developed. This is a time to appreciate where you are now, recognizing that each challenge, triumph, and lesson has brought you to this very moment. Just as Jesus called the disciples to trust Him, He calls you into a partnership that requires trust. Your past has prepared you, your present is ripe with opportunity, and your future is overflowing with promise.

Casting Your Net into the Infinite: Embracing the Journey Ahead

As we close these final pages, take a deep breath and look back at the journey we've traveled together. We began by accepting the call to cast our nets into the deep—an invitation to step beyond comfort and lean into a vision that's far bigger than ourselves. Along the way, we've peeled back layers of doubt, confronted limitations, and awakened to the truth of who we're called to be in God's kingdom.

But this journey has been about more than simply learning; it's been about transformation. We've delved into the importance of stepping boldly into our purpose, breaking free from past constraints, and creating new patterns that align with our calling. Through each chapter, we've built a framework grounded in faith, perseverance, and the courage to grow. We've discovered that true impact lies in trusting God's plan and being willing to answer His call every day.

Now, the time has come to move from reflection to action. Take a moment to examine where you've felt stuck or limited. Identify the nets you need to let go of, and step toward the expansive future waiting for you. Whether it's a single bold step or a profound reimagining of your life, commit to embracing your purpose with fresh resolve. Surround yourself with those who champion your growth, who remind you that you are capable, called, and chosen.

Remember, expanding your net is not a one-time decision; it's a lifelong journey of faith, discovery, and courage. Every day holds an invitation to expand further, to reach higher, and to live more fully aligned with the vision God has for you.

I leave you with this truth: "You were created with a purpose, and that purpose is not merely a task—it's a profound transformation." Embrace this call and let it light your path forward.

Your journey doesn't end here; it's only just beginning. Keep casting your net, pushing past the familiar into the depths of God's abundant promise. Your life is a testimony in the making—a beacon of faith, resilience, and limitless possibility.

So, go forth with courage and conviction. The extraordinary life God intended for you is right in front of you. Embrace it fully, and let your life be a radiant testament to the power of purpose.

EXPAND
YOUR NET
DECLARATION

I am a vessel of purpose, equipped with limitless potential. I embrace the journey of who I am becoming, confident that my purpose is unfolding with each step I take. I believe that God's plans for me surpass my greatest dreams. I am ready to expand my net and receive the abundance He has prepared for me. With a heart full of gratitude and anticipation, I choose to step forward, turning each moment into an opportunity to fulfill my God-given purpose. Anything that dares to stand in my way will be overcome, for God is on my side. In the powerful name of Jesus, Amen!

It's Time, Friend! ♡ Patrice M Schaffer

www.ingramcontent.com/pod-product-compliance
Lightning Source LLC
LaVergne TN
LVHW051327151224
798957LV00025BA/470/J